CHESTER MITCHELL

Sister Zeno
You are A Pearl

THE GRAVEL ROAD TO
HEAVEN

WALKING WITH GOD
THROUGH THE GRIT OF LIFE

chester mitchell
MINISTRIES

We are challenged to walk with God through the questions and crises all along the "gravel roads" that characterize this life. Sometimes the rough road of life is characterized by outer circumstances, sometimes by problems of our own making. This book encourages the believer, at every stage of growth, to journey step-by-step with God, who is always working on our behalf, the God who longs for us to know Him through His Word and through the gently whispered guidance and encouragement of His Holy Spirit.

Editorial development and creative design support by Ascent:
www.itsyourlifebethere.com

I have been blessed with a
wonderful partner on my journey!

My wife, Marion

has been my greatest source of inspiration.
Without her love, prayers, and passionate
pursuit of Christ, I would not be who I am.

My utmost joy has been the opportunity
to walk with God and have her by my side.
My constant ambition is that we will finish
this amazing journey together.

ACKNOWLEDGEMENTS

I will forever honor the memory of my spiritual father Bishop Kenneth F. Haney!

I am eternally thankful to the members of Capital Community Church who have allowed me to be their pastor for the last 16 years. Their faithfulness to God and prayers have sustained me. I am blessed to lead an amazing church.

I am grateful to the leadership team who faithfully serve our church and me: Stephen O'Donnell, Anthony Francis, Terrence Bridges, Jeff Walthall, and Jon-Paul Bellamy. I am a better leader because of their partnership. Maggie, Carol, Luz, and Valencia are invaluable assets.

Special thanks to my creative assistant Natallia Francis. Angie Fraser and Merv Levy provided valuable assistance with my drafts of the book. I am grateful to my editor Doug Wagner— his invaluable skill made the book better.

I will always cherish the great missionary to Asia, Steve Willoughby who prayed for me and declared, "I see books inside you." Without the brilliant mind and patient guidance of my writing coach, David Hazard, I would never have undertaken this project.

Finally, I am deeply indebted to my precious mother Myrtle Mitchell. Her example of walking with God has guided my life— she began her journey on the gravel roads of Robins Bay—and has inspired thousands to finish the course!

⇥ 1 ⇤

JUST BE THERE

(DON'T MISS YOUR BURNING BUSH)

One day Moses was tending the flock of his father-in-law, Jethro,
the priest of Midian. He led the flock far into the wilderness and came
to Sinai, the mountain of God. There the angel of the Lord
appeared to him in a blazing fire from the middle of a bush…Moses
stared in amazement. Though the bush was engulfed in flames,
it didn't burn up (Exodus 3:1-2—NLT).

Quite often, the portrait of our lives, as captivating as it may be to the human eye, is lacking. The canvas, the colors, the brush strokes may be ever so right, but that special "God moment" is missing. It's the moment of our calling!

The great goodness of the Good News is that we were sought by God himself and called to walk with Him.

To be clear, the idea of walking with God was never a human idea. The relationship between God and me is something that originated with God before the first brilliant crescendo of light marked the breathtaking dawn of creation. "In the beginning," the Creator desired to have intimacy with the man and woman He created. He wanted them to know Him, to love Him, to depend on Him, and to be like Him. Even in the darkest moment of the relationship—when they shivered naked and ashamed—he came walking in the garden, still calling them by name. Wherever you are today, know this: He is still calling you, just as he called Adam and Eve. He misses walking with you.

What does it mean to be called? When does it happen? Is it something I plan, or is it something God writes into the epic adventure of my unique story?

God's calling is different for each of us. For me, there was no vision, no lightning, no thunder. Just an unexpected moment when I was fully aware that God had chosen a special path for my life. My moment of calling was so sudden, so simple that I could have missed it. On the other hand, it was so awesome, so intense that it left me in tears and became a watershed moment, a moment I'll forever see in my mind.

God has chosen to deal with each of us differently. God has a moment for you just as He had one for Moses. If you'd been Moses, you would have waited 40 long years for God to show up—burning bushes don't explode into view every day. And this leads me to believe that it was a planned explosion—a controlled burn, if you will. The story of the burning bush serves as an apt metaphor for the fact that God is the one who plans the entire journey—yes, He has been planning out every aspect of your life. When good things happen, we revel in the fact that God planned it, but the same God also plans the rough and rugged parts of our walk with Him. To celebrate God only on good days is to miss Him on the many days when our hearts are broken and our spirits are crushed. You can't take God out of the picture. Neither can you remove yourself. Like Moses was, just be there!

The story of Moses' life is a reminder of just how unpredictable God is. Maybe that's why the Bible calls Him *ruach*, which means "wind" or "spirit." He moves mysteriously. John, the New Testament writer, noted that we don't know when He comes or where He's going (St John 3:8). We're never quite sure when He's going to show up. This elusive and unpredictable God has His own sense of timing and rhythm.

Waiting patiently isn't hard-wired into the human soul, so we all know what it means to become frustrated. We're impatient by nature, so a God who has His own timing and has been known to leave Moses in a desolate place for four decades doesn't quite gel with our mind-set, especially in the 21st century.

How are you doing with waiting for God? How do you react when a prayer seems to have been forgotten? How do you respond when circumstances shred your plans? How are you dealing with the sin that seemingly ambushed you in a moment when you weren't aware of your vulnerability?

When our perspective on God's sovereign plan for our lives is not properly aligned with His purpose, we become angry, embittered, and ultimately devastated. What is required on our part is a great focus. Here are a few more insights that you must embrace:

+ **Timing:** *God does nothing in the human realm that isn't in accordance with His timing. Every great and commanding movement in the drama of the human race was divinely stamped with God's timing. Even the coming of God in human form could not have happened until the "fullness of time" (Galatians 4:4) had been achieved. Every season is governed by timing. Every storm will subside eventually. No temptation is endless. "Weeping endures for a night but joy comes in the morning" (Psalm 30:5). You can trust God's timing.*

+ **Endurance:** *When you're tempted to quit, encourage yourself to keep going or seek encouragement from older, wiser believers. It's the difference between the mediocre and those who excel. Walking with God is no* *quick jog in the park. It's a daily relationship filled with divine surprises.*

♦ **Passion:** *If endurance is external, passion is internal. It's the spiritual fervor that allows us to keep moving with the same conviction with which we started. Passion keeps us from simply going through the monotonous, mind-numbing motions. Passion allows us to see our-selves finishing strong!*

The journey that we've been called to embark on will also require patience. God doesn't seem to be inclined to use a micro-wave to prepare his leaders or his children. It seems that God lets us wait because He is more concerned about the formation of our character than about our comfort. God lets us wait because He wants us to turn off our timepieces and allow Him to unfold His will just as he unfolds the flowers in the morning rain.

If you have been praying for any period of time, you know what it feels like to go from high expectations to anxiety to that sinking feeling that it's not going to happen. But consider Moses' story. He was the son of Hebrew parents who hid him in the river to save him from the genocidal edict that all male babies were to be slaughtered like animals. God allowed that special bundle of destiny to be rescued from the river. Moses became the "son of Pharaoh's daughter." He had the best of the best. He wore the finest of the finest. He was in line to become the next pharaoh of the Egyptian empire. But all that seemed so far away as he tended sheep day after day. But somewhere in heaven, things had been taking shape. The time was near, the place had been chosen, and the "bush" had grown sufficiently for the purpose that God had ordained.

Recently, I was meeting with a gifted Christian leader and listened as he poured out his heart about a ministry opportunity that hadn't worked out. He and his wife had responded to what they believed was God's leading, investing time and money, but to no avail. The doors closed, and in retrospect, it seemed that it had been a bad idea.

As we sat that day, I heard a gentle whisper, a special word from the Holy Spirit for my friend. Here is what I told him: "Stop chasing your destiny. God knows exactly where you are. In the end, your destiny will find you."

God is not inclined to move your "burning bush" to get your attention. He has already chosen the time and the place to meet with you. Your responsibility is simply to be there.

A STEP ON THE JOURNEY:

Recognize God not only as the Lord of your destiny or ultimate purpose but also as the Lord of your daily life. Involve God in daily decisions such as:

+ *How will I respond to this problem?*

+ *How will I deal with this person?*

+ *What words of encouragement will I speak?*

+ *Who is in need of my prayers today?*

+ *What lie or distortion about my identity will I no longer believe?*

A PRAYER:

Dear Heavenly Father, thank you for choosing me for divine assignments. Thank you for trusting me to walk faithfully with you during the "wilderness seasons." Give me the wisdom to resist the distractions of daily life, the insignificant things that lead me away from my "burning bush." By your grace, I want to be there. I want to stand on holy ground and allow my destiny to find me! Amen.

2

POINT OF NO RETURN

(WHEN YOU'RE CAUGHT BETWEEN FAITH AND FEAR)

Camp Highroad is one of those places I won't soon forget—hundreds of beautiful acres of God's creation in the quaint Virginia town of Middleburg. I had come to join with a wonderful group of Godly men to experience God's presence and share a great time of fellowship. Friday evening's speaker was outstanding, and I was thankful for what was shaping up to be a very spiritual and relaxing time. This retreat from the world was going exactly as I wanted it to go—no challenges, no stress, just peace and an easy time. For the moment, I was unaware of the challenges that lay just ahead.

Unknown to me, long before time began, God had destined that I would learn a valuable lesson at this moment of my life. All too often we expect life, and our walk through it with God, to be easy. We expect that because He is our loving Heavenly Father, He will deliver us from our problems. While he can, quite often he chooses to lead us through the experiences of life, painful as well as pleasurable. This is where walking with God becomes meaningful and intimacy is born. Somewhere in the middle of the journey, we discover the Christ that we so desperately long to know. We know Him, really know Him!

So there I was, enjoying the tranquility of the country and the peace of a weekend retreat, and somewhere up in heaven God must have been smiling at me because he knew that the next morning my peaceful mind-set would quickly fade. It was Saturday morning, and after breakfast, prayer, and another inspiring talk we headed up the path away from the lodge for our recreation time. We divided into two teams, one bound for the archery range and the other for the zip line. By the time I'd fully processed what the zip line was—a plunge through free space while tethered to a ridiculously thin wire—I was headed up the hill to the staging area, where the harnesses lay on the floor. "There has to be a 'spiritual' and gracious way for a senior pastor to pass," I thought, groping for a way out. "Surely a group of Christian men would allow their leader to bow out of this silly little exercise."

As I looked around at the group, which included some seriously buff alpha males and real daredevils, I realized that there were actually *three* groups. Group 1 consisted of the men who seemingly had no fear, their blood pumping at the opportunity to jump off the staging area and zip down through the trees attached to a simple harness fastened to a line. Group 2 were the guys pursing their lips. These were the boys who were going to do it not because they were "born to be wild" but because they wanted to prove to themselves that they could face down fear. And then there was group 3. These were the men who were desperately afraid. These were the men who weren't ready to die. No gift of discernment was needed to see that these were the guys who, if given just a small window of opportunity to head back down the mountain to a safe place, they would have. They had no shame about the fact that they wanted out. I was a charter member of group 3.

As I stood there with the beads of sweat coming down my face, I realized that this situation was just like so many of the daunting challenges we face in trying to walk through life with God. Walking with God will require you to step out onto the edge of your fear. It will demand that you entrust someone else with your life, with your very future. The story unfolds only when you choose to override your fears with the faith that you aren't the first and you won't be the last to step across the line into God's favorite place—where He is totally in control. Others have taken the journey you are about to embark on and have arrived at the end of the line with an unshakable confidence in a God who will not allow you to fall. Walking with God is all about letting go of what you think and listening to the One who knows more because He is committed to not just the beginning of the journey but your safe arrival in heaven.

If today finds you standing at the point of no return, consider God's promise to you:

> *Now all glory to God, who is able to keep you from falling away and will bring you with great joy into his glorious presence without a single fault. All glory to him who alone is God, our Savior through Jesus Christ our Lord. All glory, majesty, power, and authority are his before all time, and in the present, and beyond all time! Amen (Jude 24-25—NLT).*

It is time to make the decision—the decision to place our lives in the control of someone who we absolutely believe has the ability to keep us safe.

In the forty years since I have been not only a Christian but a leader of others, I have come to understand that walking with God is indeed much like stepping off a platform into the air, with challenges sometimes rushing at you faster than you can handle.

And all the while you're being asked to trust in something that's supposed to be there to hold you up, help you face down your fears, and maybe even help you relax and enjoy the "ride" of life. Let's face it, transferring trust to someone you don't know is never easy. And that's why walking with God is so vital—somewhere along the journey, He challenges us to let go and allow Him to be Lord!

Of all the Psalms, there is none to compare to the rhythmic simplicity and the enormous encouragement of Psalm 23. How could David have known that a simple song born of his many moments' challenges would inspire generations of people to experience life from its many touch points?

Walking with God will indeed require you to "step off." This is where you trust your weight to God's faithfulness. These are the moments when we go against our instinctive desire to lean on our own understanding. Walking with God will often involve dealing with the unknown—we walk with God even though we don't know where we're going. In the words of Corrie Ten Boom, who was able to live out her faith in a Nazi concentration camp in spite of the constant threat of death, "Never be afraid to trust an unknown future to a known God."

Just like my zip line experience, walking with God is about tension. What we know about the God of the Bible is totally different from what we know when we are knowing God during real-time, real-life experiences. We read that God is our provider, but it's when the factory you've relied on for income has been moved to Mexico and your job is gone that we know that God is our true source of provision. As we walk with Him, the God of the Bible becomes our lifelong companion, and ultimately we learn to act on what has been revealed in the Bible because we know the author personally!

Walking with God is challenging because we were created by God *for* God. He is more committed to a relationship with you than you are to Him. Everyone who has ever walked with Him faithfully has come away with gratitude for the opportunity to share such a breathtaking experience and a desire to do it again!

A verse spoke to me as I stood there eyeing the zip line: "Even when the way goes through Death Valley, I'm not afraid when you walk at my side. Your trusty shepherd's crook makes me feel secure" (Psalm 23:4—The Message). The gutsy group 1 guys were jockeying for position to see who would go first. The group 2 guys with the steely eyes stood in the middle, more or less ready. And the group 3 guys were visibly shaken. And it was at that moment that I made the decision to bypass group 2 and step up with the group 1 crazies.

Why? If I was ever going to do it, I needed to do it before my window of courage closed. It was closing rapidly! Yes, I prayed. Yes, I quickly reflected on the wonderful life I'd lived. I was ready to do something that nothing in my physical being wanted to do, but in my spirit I knew I had to do it. I was surrounded by a "cloud of witnesses"—other believing men—who needed to see a living example of what it means to walk with God. Or in this case, to zip line with God.

Just before the guide unhooked me from the tree, he said, "Do you want to go off gradually or do you want to jump?" I didn't answer, because at that moment, I was at peace. I had placed my life, one more time, in God's ever-uplifting hands.

And I stepped off into thin air, onto nothingness.

Everyone has to find himself or herself. To be a group 3 individual is fine. That's who you are and this is where you are now. You can never begin a journey with God until you come to some key realizations:

✦ *I might be afraid, but God is my shepherd.*

✦ *No matter what happens, I will have the Holy Spirit's help.*

✦ *God will be with me every step of the way.*

✦ *At the end of my journey, I will have my own personal Psalm 23. It will be the story of a God who walked with me in difficult places. It will be my song about the times when God gave me the courage to keep going when everything inside me screamed, "Stop!"*

As I have reflected on my "jumping off" moment, I can still remember the rush. A funny thing happened in that moment. I was no longer afraid. I found myself enjoying the thrill of the ride. I was grateful that that this "group 3" pastor had faced his fears one more time.

A STEP ON THE JOURNEY:

Take the next seven days and read all of Psalm 23 each morning before you begin your day and read it again before you go to sleep. If you've memorized the words, as I have, you'll be tempted to rush through it. Don't. Think about each verse deeply. Allow it to saturate your mind and your heart. Reflect on a challenge, a crisis, an anxiety that you're dealing with or will face in the near future, and allow the song to become your anthem of victory. If you're facing a season of pain and find yourself wishing you could back out of it, I want to assure you that God will not let you fall. If you're facing a loss and dreading that feeling of dangling, please know that you have an untapped reserve of strength and courage that will sustain you until the next season comes.

One last word: Everyone in the group jumped. A few of the guys told me, "Pastor, when I saw you jump, I decided that I would."

During our time together, we will be looking at the lives of people just like you and me. Some pushed off gently, while others jumped, but they all walked with God. Who knows—maybe someone will do it because you did. All the people of faith found in Hebrews chapter 11 did it. They're cheering you on!

Do you see what this means—all these pioneers who blazed the way, all these veterans cheering us on (Hebrews 12:1— The Message).

~3~

IS THERE ANYONE OUT THERE?

(Seeing the Invisible)

Hope is the word which God has written
on the brow of every man.—Victor Hugo

Type the name *Carl Sagan* into Google and you'll find the story of a legendary American astronomer. Somewhere in his bio, you'll also find that he lived from 1934 to 1996 and died without any hope for the afterlife. Here's what his widow wrote after his passing:

> *Contrary to the fantasies of the fundamentalists, there was no deathbed conversion, no last-minute refuge taken in a comforting vision of a heaven or an afterlife. For Carl, what mattered most was what was true, not merely what would make us feel better. Even at this moment when anyone would be forgiven for turning away from the reality of our situation, Carl was unflinching. As we looked deeply into each other's eyes, it was with a shared conviction that our wondrous life together was ending forever.[1]*

Walking with God today is not only about today–it is also about tomorrow. As humans, we want to know what future holds for us. Man was not made only with a temporary body but also with an eternal soul; thus we instinctively wonder about eternal matters. But for Carl Sagan, there was no future, because he believed that the sum total of life was connected to a human body. He had no hope!

What is this thing called hope? Quite often, we use the word in a casual way. We say, "I hope things will work out," or, "I hope that when I die, I'll go to heaven." But what we mean is more like "I wish things would work out" or "I'd really like them to work out." In spite of all our technological, scientific, and social advances, something is missing from our modern definition of hope.

A definition of true biblical hope might read like this: confident expectation that God will always act consistently in agreement with His Word, His Will, and His Character. It is confidence in God, both in the present and in the afterlife!

As you face life's challenges, hope will allow you to deal with them on the basis of faith rather than fear. Hope will allow you to find creative solutions because you fundamentally believe what God has spoken in His Word. Here are some words of hope from God's Word: "According to my earnest expectation and my hope, that in nothing I shall be ashamed, but that with all boldness, as always, so now also Christ shall be magnified in my body, whether it be by life or by death" (Ephesians 1:20).

Do you sense the hope in Paul's spirit? In Romans 8:28, Paul speaks with confidence, standing on facts that God has revealed about Himself as He walks alongside us. These are the facts: No matter what happens, God is my Father. He is always looking out for my good. I have a written guarantee from Him that somewhere in the future, I will be able to look back at today and see the good that has come out of what seemed to be a painful season.

And we know that God causes everything to work together for the good of those who love God and are called according to his purpose for them (Romans 8:28—NLT).

We fix our gaze on things that cannot be seen. For the things we see now will soon be gone, but the things we cannot see will last forever (2 Corinthians 4:18—NLT).

For we know that when this earthly tent we live in is taken down (that is, when we die and leave this earthly body), we will have a house in heaven, an eternal body made for us by God himself and not by human hands (2 Corinthians 5:1—NLT).

Let's look at Philippians 1:20: "For I fully expect and hope that I will never be ashamed, but that I will continue to be bold for Christ, as I have been in the past. And I trust that my life will bring honor to Christ, whether I live or die."

It's important to understand that this letter wasn't written from a comfortable resort. It was written from a damp, dark, dingy Roman prison. Take the time to read this brief letter and take note of how many times the author uses the word *joy.*

Where did this joy come from? Paul hopes and expects that he will not be ashamed. He has an unshakable confidence that Christ will be magnified regardless of whether he lives or dies. Do you have this hope? The good news is that it's available to you.

Recently, *Time* magazine did a story about the human brain titled "The Optimism Bias." Researchers found that the human brain is "wired for hope" and concluded that it was created not simply to store memories but also to create images of what the future could and should be.[2]

Each day God invites you and me to walk with Him through what seems like a hopeless situation. Have you ever paused to reflect on the life of the patriarch Abraham? His life was a journey of faith. God initiated a relationship with Abraham in Genesis 12 by inviting the pagan Bedouin to leave Ur of the Chaldees and all that was familiar and go searching for a land he had never seen. Far from perfect, Abraham had moments that lead us to wonder if God could have chosen someone better. Why did God call Abraham "friend"? The most powerful lesson to be learned from the life of Abraham is that God, too, is looking. He's searching for someone who will simply believe what God has already spoken!

Maybe today finds you in the same predicament as Abraham. God told Abraham that his seed would be like the star-studded night sky and like the innumerable grains of sand in the sea. Caught in this powerful predicament, the aged father had to embrace a promise that seemed impossible to keep. Here's my favorite rendition of the verses:

> We call Abraham "father" not because he got God's attention by living like a saint, but because God made something out of Abraham when he was a nobody. Isn't that what we've always read in Scripture, God saying to Abraham, "I set you up as father of many peoples"? Abraham was first named "father" and then became a father because he dared to trust God to do what only God could do: raise the dead to life, with a word

make something out of nothing. When everything was hope-
less, Abraham believed anyway, deciding to live not on the
basis of what he saw he couldn't do but on what God said he
would do. And so he was made father of a multitude of peoples.
God himself said to him, "You're going to have a big family,
Abraham!" Abraham didn't focus on his own impotence and
say, "It's hopeless. This hundred-year-old body could never
father a child." Nor did he survey Sarah's decades of infertility
and give up. He didn't tiptoe around God's promise asking
cautiously skeptical questions. He plunged into the promise
and came up strong, ready for God, sure that God would make
good on what he had said (Romans 4:17-21—The Message).

Ultimately, hope is about reliance. Think about all the pre-
scriptions you've received from your pharmacist. You probably
didn't understand what your doctor had written. The pharmacist handed you pills that you might not have been familiar with.
You confidently took them, expecting to get better. In the same
manner, if God has given His promise, it will come to pass even
when you don't understand or even when your feelings don't
correspond to your faith. True hope is never wishy-washy or
vague. "Gee, I wish this would happen" is not the language of
hope. Hope is what we know for sure. It is the unshakable belief
that God is utterly trustworthy. The hope that the Bible teaches
is both a hope *in* God and a hope *for* an eternity with Christ.

It's amazing how many people live in fear, doubt, and anxiety.
You are God's child—whatever challenges you face, just remember that your heavenly Father loves you at your best and at your
worst. He just loves you!

Carl Sagan looked into the heavens and saw stars, but he
didn't believe there was someone out there. We who are believers
see beyond the stars. We see a bright future waiting for us.

There is far more here than meets the eye. The things we see now are here today, gone tomorrow. But the things we can't see now will last forever (2 Corinthians 4:18—The Message).

A STEP ON THE JOURNEY:

Commit to memorizing and meditating on verses in the Bible that keep your hope alive:

Don't let your hearts be troubled. Trust in God, and trust also in me. There is more than enough room in my Father's home. If this were not so, would I have told you that I am going to prepare a place for you? When everything is ready, I will come and get you, so that you will always be with me where I am. And you know the way to where I am going (St John 14:1-14—NLT).

4

THE WAITING ROOM

(THE PLACE OF SPIRITUAL FORMATION)

A strange thing happened to me while I was in my doctor's waiting room, waiting for the nurse to call me in for my yearly physical.

"Have you cut back on your sugar?" I could hear Dr. Bruce ask in my mind.

"Yes."

"Have you been exercising regularly?"

"Yes."

"Any problems since I last saw you?"

"No."

But unknown to me, I was sabotaging myself even as that reassuring imaginary conversation played out. When the nurse checked my blood pressure, she frowned. The reading was 189 over 85. I was not happy. "Major equipment failure," I thought. Not what I expected. At her suggestion, I breathed deeply several times and cleared my mind. Five minutes later, the second reading was 135 over 71. What was the problem?

The nurse explained that some people sit in the waiting room and allow their minds to cause them stress as they wait. I hadn't been aware of it, but I'd been a victim of the waiting room.

My situation—my problem—was of my own making. I had allowed a place of rest to become a place of stress.

What do you do while you're waiting for your divine assignment? I would encourage you to first allow God to work on your character. There's simply no substitute for the time we spend just allowing Christ to be formed in us. Take the time to read verses like Isaiah 40:31—NKJV: "But those who wait on the LORD shall renew their strength; They shall mount up with wings like eagles, They shall run and not be weary, They shall walk and not faint."

In Exodus chapter 3, Moses has been in the waiting room not for four minutes or four hours—he has been waiting to be ushered into God's presence for 40 years.

Let's face the truth, waiting is not an American virtue. Our culture hands us one gadget after another, each one supposed to operate faster than the last. You know the feeling: The latest upgrade comes out and suddenly you realize how slow the last one was. No one wants a slower iPhone, iPad, iPod, or any other "iGadget." Faster is better!

Is it?

Have you fallen prey to the instant-success syndrome? You do so when you assume that greatness is the work of one magical moment. Take away the 40 years in the dry, barren, lonely desert and the man who led millions of people out of Egypt wouldn't have been the Moses that we know. Take away the loneliness you're experiencing right now and a vital part of God's design for your life will be missing. Take away the brokenness and the many nights that you cried because of the revealing of your secret sin and the resulting shame—as Moses did—and the required tenderness would be missing when you walk among others who are broken.

Moses was ready to represent God before the Pharaoh because he had walked with God in a place so many have resisted: the waiting room! God had chosen Moses, and God has chosen you. There is a divine assignment for which we are all born, and the waiting room has always been the place where spiritual formation takes place. It's the place where God leaves us in order to test us. The idea of walking with God should not be taken to mean literal human movement. Walking with God speaks about the unique process that God chooses, the events He places in your path to teach you how to respond in a godly manner. This is how God develops you for the purpose He designed for you long ago.

> For we are God's masterpiece. He has created us anew in Christ Jesus, so we can do the good things he planned for us long ago (Ephesians 2:10—NLT).

If this season finds you in a "wilderness," I encourage you to seek God's perspective and resist the temptation to think that He has abandoned you. He knows exactly where you are, and He will speak clearly when it's time to initiate your assignment.

Moses was about to discover that the God of his destiny was ready to become the Lord of his daily life. This is the essence of walking with God. Each day as Moses led the Jews, he understood that he needed to place his faith in the God who came down in the burning bush. This is the same God who would open the Red Sea. This is the same God who would cause water to rush out of granite-like rock. This is the same God who will perform miracle after miracle as you journey with Him.

We wait for God by prayerfully asking Him to deal with the "character flaws" in our lives. Instead of becoming angry at the passing of the days, use this moment to ask your heavenly Father to prepare your heart for His next assignment for you.

Pray this prayer:

God, while I am waiting for You, use this moment to teach me grace. Use this season to teach me how to walk in humility so that You will be able to trust me with bigger responsibilities. I ask You today to prepare me to hear Your voice so that I will know how to respond in the days ahead when the pressure is increased. Amen.

As a pastor and counselor, I am often asked the secret to knowing God's voice. I have found that many times God's will in our lives begins as a small seed. It is embryonic in its essence. God's big assignment for your life begins today with the impression that you have to invite the moms in the neighborhood over for tea and cookies on a regular basis. It begins with the seed thought that you could make a big difference in the lives of the young boys in the neighborhood by teaching them how to fish the same way the man in your neighborhood did for you after your dad passed away many years ago. Have you noticed that you're driven to your knees in prayer for missionaries?

The waiting room filled me with unnecessary anxiety. Quite often, we miss God's will for us because while we're waiting, we focus on all the reasons why God could never make something great out of our lives. During his 40 years in the waiting room, Moses had to settle the issues of his past. He had killed a man in the heat of the moment. Had God forgiven him? Had this mistake derailed God's purpose in his life? What about the fact that he lacked the oratorical skills we associate with great leaders? Ironically, after 40 years in the wilderness, Moses still felt inadequate to speak on behalf of God.

Here's what I now know: The waiting room is not about my becoming perfect. It's the place where God prepares me so He can accomplish something through me.

When at last you emerge from the wilderness, let it be with a confidence that whatever God has asked you to do, wherever God would choose to send you, let there be the confidence in your heart that God will empower you. God will speak through you. And in the end, everyone will know that you were simply God's earthly instrument in a drama that was written and orchestrated in heaven.

My prayer is that you will rid yourself of the instant-success mentality and allow God's timing to be worked out in your life. Who knows—any day now the ordinary just might become extraordinary, the mundane might become majestic, and the parched clay might become holy ground. Right where you stand, thinking you're doing nothing but "waiting."

Ultimately, we will realize that our creator ordained every day of our lives. You haven't missed God's will. You're simply being prepared for something beyond your wildest imagination. Breathe deeply!

A STEP ON THE JOURNEY:

1. *Ask God to give you His perspective about His timing in your life.*

2. *Reaffirm your commitment to developing a particular character quality while you're waiting.*

I pray that your hearts will be flooded with light so that you can understand the confident hope he has given to those he called-his holy people who are his rich and glorious inheritance (Ephesians 1:19—NLT).

Therefore I, a prisoner for serving the LORD, beg you to lead a life worthy of your calling, for you have been called by God (Ephesians 4:1—NLT).

~5~

ARE WE
THERE YET?

(GOD IS STILL WORKING ON ME)

I'm not saying that I have this all together, that I have it made.
But I am well on my way, reaching out for Christ, who has so wondrously
reached out for me. Friends, don't get me wrong: By no means do I count
myself an expert in all of this, but I've got my eyes on the goal, where God
is beckoning us onward—to Jesus (Philippians 3:12-14—The Message).

Paul is the poster child for all of us who are in the middle of our walk with God. He has benefited from a spectacular conversion and a miraculous restoration of his sight, as recorded in Acts 9. Like many of us, he finds himself in an unexpected place, unsure of what the future holds. But *unlike* many of us, in spite of his circumstances, he speaks with expectation, joy, and hope about the future. He's leveraging his past and dispensing with distractions, all the while focusing on what's ahead. One word sums up his passion: *onward.*

I recently spoke with Rob (not his real name), one of the most gifted Christians I've ever met. To be honest, I've repented a time or two of the sin of jealousy as I've watched the Holy Spirit use him to inspire God's people. He has a unique gift that few people have. But it didn't take long to realize that the man on the stage was different from the man behind the mask. As we talked, layer after layer revealed someone who was far removed from whom he once was. Sure, the "church language" was still fluent, the gifting still evident, and he hadn't committed one of the "big" sins. He was still very much in love with his wife. All the important pieces of his life seemed to be in place, but *something* was missing.

For some, the missing piece is the decision to stop doing "for" Christ and embracing the commitment to spend time "with" Christ. For others, the missing piece is dealing with the pain that comes from a relationship that has careened off the tracks and lies in a thousand pieces. Every relationship with God will have a moment when the human aspect of the relationship must be laid to rest. Many years ago, I read these words and committed them to memory:

> *God who gives the beginning,*
> *Gives the end,*
> *A place for broken things,*
> *Too broke to mend!*

Right now, your spiritual GPS might be indicating that you are, in the words of Bono, "stuck in a moment and you can't get out of it." You're in the middle of what began as an exciting and awe-inspiring walk with God. You're like the sparkling classic convertible sitting in the middle of the mall. It's impressive on the outside, but under the hood, the battery has lost it power.

If you're like me, you can relate to Psalm 73. It's the brooding of a disillusioned soul, a man who must reconcile a "good God" and the fact that bad people seem to get a "free ride":

No doubt about it! God is good—good to good people, good to the good-hearted. But I nearly missed it, missed seeing his goodness. I was looking the other way, looking up to the people at the top, envying the wicked who have it made (Psalm 73:1-4 The Message).

The turning point in the psalmist's season of confusion comes in the middle of the psalm: "Still, when I tried to figure it out, all I got was a splitting headache.... Until I entered the sanctuary of God. Then I saw the whole picture" (Psalm 73:16-17).

The last verse of Psalm 73 reminds us that we must continue to walk with God in spite of our limited understanding of what God is doing, that things make sense only when we are in His presence: "But I'm in the very presence of God—oh, how refreshing it is! I've made Lord God my home. God, I'm telling the world what you do!" (Psalm 73:28—The Message.)

All of us can remember the ecstasy of first love—those were the days when you could hardly wait to pray. The tears of repentance fell like summer rain, but not just out of your eyes—it was much deeper than that. The soil of your heart was saturated with moisture, and so you wept out of your innermost being.

Those were the days when God's Word—literally every word—was precious. You didn't need a theological definition. You walked in simple obedience because conviction came easily. Back then you didn't notice the rules, because you didn't need them. Walking with God was inspired by "fire in your bones" (Jeremiah 20:9 KJV).

What happened to *that* person? That's the question we all ponder. Suddenly we have to deal with the fact that in our walk with God, we took it for granted that the initial burst of passion would be sufficient to go the distance. Somewhere along the journey, we bought into the notion that the "feeling phase" would never end. And now we find ourselves asking, "Are we there yet?"

The history of God's relationship with the children of Israel is an appropriate metaphor for New Testament Christians. Study the history of the varied kings and you notice the same story being repeated time and time again: A young king takes the throne. In the tender years of his leadership, he serves the Lord and walks passionately in the Lord's commandment. Somewhere in the middle, something changes in his heart and he veers like a car out of control. He walks away from the person he once was and the relationship he once had. You hear it in God's reminder to King Saul: "When you were little in your own eyes..." (1 Samuel 15:17).

One of the most important keys to walking with God over a long period of time is an appreciation for times of renewal. Everything in the created universe requires renewal. Trees renew themselves, eagles shed old feathers to make way for the new, salmon fight the current to return to their birthplace to prepare for new life. A careful examination of the Christian Church reveals that its finest moments were the times when the dying embers of religious tradition felt the fresh breath of the Holy Spirit and the Church experienced a spiritual awakening—a renaissance, if you will.

When was the last time you stopped the merry-go-round of religious activity? Better yet, when was the last time you became so desperate that you took the risk and simply jumped off? Walking with God ceases to be a merry-go-round when we lose our passion.

Create in me a clean heart, O God and renew a steadfast spirit within me. Do not cast me away from your presence, And do not take Your Holy Spirit from me. Restore to me the

*joy of your salvation, And uphold me by Your generous Spirit
(Psalm 51:10-12—NKJV).*

If today finds you out of spiritual fuel, going through the
motions while dreading the journey, God has a message for you:
This moment is not unique to you. David experienced it and
shared his experience in a song. We find the words in Psalm 63:

*O God, you are my God; Early will I seek You; My soul
thirst for You; My flesh longs for You in a dry and thirsty
land where there is not water. So I have looked for You in the
sanctuary. To see Your power and Your glory. Because Your
loving-kindness is better than life, My lips shall praise You.
Thus I will bless You while I live; I will lift up my hands in
Your name (Psalm 63:1-4).*

Take a moment to notice how many times David uses the
words *You* and *Your.*

David is a desperate man intentionally refocusing. He has
made the decision to allow good things, necessary things, evil
things, and even urgent things to go out of focus so that he can
focus on the most important thing. For you, that one thing is a
daily relationship with Christ.

I concluded my visit with my friend Rob by challenging him
to move away from doing "churchy" work and spend time with
the Christ who loves the Church and desires a private and public
love affair with him. I reminded him that when Paul wrote to the
Christians at Rome, "Be not conformed ... but be transformed,"
He intentionally structured his words to indicate that transformation happens when we present ourselves, just as a weary,
mud-drenched farmer presents himself to the shower at the
end of a back-breaking day in the field. Transformation is also

something we allow God (the Living Water) to do to us. The best of us will fail if walking with God doesn't involve a partnership with the Holy Spirit. Finally, transformation is indicated by the Greek tense to be something that happens continually.

That morning I reminded Rob, and myself, that activity, even religious activity, is empty if it's devoid of spiritual renaissance.

Make this your prayer: "Won't you revive us again, so your people can rejoice in you?" (Psalm 85:6—NLT).

Wherever you are in your walk with God, it's important that you continually remain open to the work of the Holy Spirit because transformation is the process of a lifetime lived in a walk with God.

> *But friends, that's exactly who we are: children of God. And that's only the beginning. Who knows how we'll end up! What we know is that when Christ is openly revealed, we'll see him— and in seeing him, become like him. All of us who look forward to his Coming stay ready, with the glistening purity of Jesus' life as a model for our own (1 John 3:2-3—The Message).*

The Christian life was never meant to be easy. Unexpected moments are built into the journey. Contrary to what the culture teaches, difficulties are not meant to make us question God. They are opportunities for our Heavenly Father to move us closer to the goal of being like Him.

A STEP ON THE JOURNEY:

Meditate on Philippians 3:

1. Practice a new way of thinking.
2. Push through every obstacle.
3. Position yourself to focus on an eternal reward.

∞ **6** ∞

"DIY" DISASTER

(HOME IMPROVEMENT GOD'S WAY)

*There has never been the slightest doubt in my mind that the God
who started this great work in you would keep at it and bring it
to a flourishing finish on the very day Christ Jesus appears
(Philippians 1:6—The Message).*

As Americans, we love to roll up our sleeves and "do it
ourselves." We have an entire television channel, the **DIY
Network,** dedicated to helping us tackle projects on our own,
without having to rely on professional help. Rightfully so, we
feel a sense of pride after mastering new skills and empowering
ourselves to build or fix something around the house.

Several years ago my wife Marion and I were excited to move
into a larger home. It was in a great neighborhood with beautiful
landscaping and a quiet cul-de-sac. Immediately after moving
in, the restless type A inside me decided that the basement space
needed to be finished. It was the craziest idea, but at the time
it seemed to be a "God idea." Looking back, I know now that
God ideas, good ideas and goofy ideas swim in the same stream
and it can be traumatic if you mistake one for the other. Sadly, I
mistook one for another. This wasn't a God idea or even a good
idea. Not even close.

Here I was, a guy who knows nothing about construction, a guy who never met a tool he liked, a husband who, if anything needs repairing in his house, asks his wife to fix it—here I was undertaking the massive task of finishing a large basement.

Needless to say, the project was beyond me. For several months, I became friends with all the salespeople at the local Home Depot; they called me by my first name because I was their most regular customer. Everyone in the store was rooting for me because they felt sorry for this non-builder who had taken on a job he wasn't equipped to handle by himself.

While initiative and self-reliance are admirable traits, sooner or later we encounter a project that dwarfs our amateur abilities. In these moments, the wise course of action is to ask for help. Yet sometimes, in our stubborn independence, we refuse to admit our need for aid, choosing to press on alone. As the television show *DIY Disasters* attests, our attempts at self-sufficiency routinely backfire. Many of our remodeling projects end up in ruins, leaving property badly damaged. But at least Americans can take solace in knowing we're not alone. Christians have our own DIY disaster stories.

The world tells us we have what it takes to do it ourselves and do it now, but God instructs us to form ourselves in His image. This is not a DIY project. There can be no success if you don't show up, but as you well know, you alone will never be enough. The grand designer of the human species factored into the design specifications that something from outside ourselves would be essential if we're to reach our redemptive potential. One is too small a number for success!

Have you kept a secret that has you imprisoned on the edge of spiritual self destruction? Have you caught yourself saying,

"I can handle_____"? Have you learned how to live as a functional_____?

How do we move from independence to God-dependence and then to interdependence? Here are a few key steps:

1. *Confess a "secret sin" to a mature Christian who will cover you with prayer and grace.*

2. *Ask someone to help you with an addiction you are attempting to break.*

3. *Make a commitment to become sensitive to the Holy Spirit's cautions by dealing with the flashing yellow lights before they become red lights!*

For many Christians, what begins as a commitment to walk with God over time comes to resemble Chester Mitchell standing in the middle of a dust-filled basement wondering why in the world his loving wife didn't give him a sedative the moment he mentioned doing it on his own. Just like Marion did, God stands on the sidelines and allows us to charge off on our own, but he never loses sight of us, because He knows we won't be able to do it on our own.

> *I am the Vine, you are the branches. When you're joined with me and I with you, the relation intimate and organic, the harvest is sure to be abundant. Separated, you can't produce a thing (John 15:5—The Message).*

What are the challenges you're facing in your life? Many of us struggle to demonstrate the love of Christ in our relationships when our natural instinct is to allow our anger to rule. Place a "d" in front of the *anger* and you get *danger*. We know that anger is dangerous, but we still struggle to keep it under control. If you're like me, you want to ask St. Paul about that "be angry

" verse when you get to heaven. He must have meant
and repent later." That version has worked for me
. But seriously, why would God give us the capacity
for anger and then ask us to build healthy relationships where
anger doesn't destroy the foundation like an infestation of deadly
termites? He knew it was possible, just not on our own.

Or maybe your challenge is your relationship. You thought
you could fix it, but with the passing of time, its condition has
grown worse. You now find yourself wondering if you should
have refrained from confronting the issues. Or maybe you're
locked in a vise of depression over your finances. With the
passing of each month you're sinking deeper and deeper into
a quagmire of red ink. In the beginning you thought, "Surely
I can handle this without alarming my husband." But you were
wrong, and now you're ashamed and trapped in a prison of fear.

Or maybe everything in your life seemed normal and routine
until a routine visit to your family doctor caused your world
to implode. He walked in and gave you the news: cancer. The
news pierced your heart like a dagger. You hadn't planned to be
divorced and single in this season of your life, and now cancer
has assaulted your body. Whatever you're facing, you may sense
that you're alone, but you're not. Jesus Christ is with you, right
here and right now.

In the darkest moments of our lives, we're tempted to snatch
the control mechanisms away from God in a futile and self-de-
structive attempt at "self-navigation." During my traumatic
season as a builder, though, I quickly realized I needed help from
people I didn't know but whom I was forced to trust. The electri-
cian knew what was required for the project to pass the county
inspection. I trusted him and the project passed the inspection.
The plumber knew exactly what to do—I stood back and trusted

him. He got it right, and so did the other subcontractors who helped me. My desire to control everything had to be suppressed because I had taken on a project that I lacked the essential skills to finish on my own. Walking with God will frustrate you and frustrate the work of God in you unless you make the decision again and again to trust him.

Here's how successful pastor and Christian author Craig Groeschel described himself:

> At the age of twenty-five, I was a full-time pastor and a part-time follower of Christ. Does any of this resonate with your experience? Was there a time in your life that you were closer to God than you are today? If you're like me, your spiritual drift didn't happen on purpose. Like a tiny leak in a tire, slowly but surely, your spiritual passion quietly slipped away. Maybe it has just become clear to you. Instead of a fully devoted follower of Christ, you've unintentionally become a full-time mom or full-time student or a full-time bank clerk— and a part-time follower of Christ.

Groschell identified himself as a "Christian Atheist—someone who professes that Christ exists but lives as if everything depends on them!"[3]

You trusted God at the start of the relationship, in the days when you didn't have much. But now you have much more at stake, and while it's harder to trust Him now, the need for that trust is greater than ever.

> Trust in the Lord with all you, heart, And lean not on your own understanding; In all your ways acknowledge Him, And He shall direct your path (Proverbs 3:5-6—NKJV).

In other words, don't attempt to walk with God by listening to your head. More on this from Lamentations et al.:

Your head tells you that you have failed, but your heart tells you to get up and try again. Your head tells you that God stopped loving you the last time you sinned, but your heart tells you "His mercies are new every morning." (Lamentations 3:22-23)

Your head tells you that you can make it on your own but your heart tells you "God is my refuge and my strength" (Psalm 46:1).

Your head tells you to hide your weakness and pretend that you can do it on your own, but your heart tells you that God's strength becomes perfect in your weakness (2 Corinthians 12:9).

The years have passed since I mistook that goofy idea for a God idea. Friends and family now descend the stairs to admire the work. To be honest, I'm surprised at how well it turned out. Would I do it again? Yes! Because I now know that if you have the right plan and the right people—if you have the right help—something beautiful will emerge from the chaos. How? The answer is in Philippians: "I can do all things through him who gives me strength" (Philippians 4:13—NIV).

Speaking of help, here's what Jesus said before He left:

But the Helper, the Holy Spirit, whom the Father will send in My name, He will teach you all things, and bring to your remembrance all things that I said to you. Peace I leave with you, My peace I give to you; not as the world gives do I give to you. Let not your heart be troubled, neither let it be afraid (John 14:26-27—NKJV).

And this: "Nevertheless I tell you the truth. It is to your advantage that I go away; for if I do not go away the Helper will not come to you; but if I depart, I will send Him to you" (John 16:7—NKJV).

A STEP ON THE JOURNEY:

Pray this prayer of repentance:

Father, I have tried to walk with You without understanding my need for God and others. In so doing, I have offended You because You placed me in the Church—Your body—so I would not be alone. I confess that I have allowed my pride and the desire to be independent to empower Satan's attack. Give me grace to walk in humility and interdependence. In Jesus' name! Amen.

Make a list of three people you will personally share your weaknesses with and invite them to pray for you daily and hold you accountable.

Two people are better off than one, for they can help each other succeed. If one person falls, the other can reach out and help. But someone who falls alone is in real trouble (Ecclesiastes 4:9-10—NLT).

Ask God to place you in circumstances that will require you to have a greater dependence on the Holy Spirit and less dependence on your own ability.

⇥ 7 ⇤

READY, SET, GO

(The Joy Is in the Journey)

Enoch lived a total of 365 years, He walked steadily with God.
And then one day he was simply gone: God took him
(Genesis 5:23-24—The Message).

Ask a group of believers what it means to walk with God and you'll hear a myriad of answers. Some of them will be spot-on, while others may cause you to wonder.

For some it's the mistaken idea that walking with God is equivalent to having your own personal Santa Claus who's only job is to make sure you get exactly what you want. God becomes the fat, jolly man who's concerned about making you happy. It's the gospel of "come, follow me and I'll guarantee that you always have the biggest and brightest and the latest *iDevice.*"

For others, walking with God is indelibly branded with the idea of giving up everything. While this is a biblical concept, the "god" they embrace is primarily about making sure you don't enjoy life. If it's fun, it can't be spiritual. If it brings happiness, it should be viewed with suspicion. Walking with God becomes much like walking with the Grinch who stole Christmas.

No doubt, you've met people for whom walking with God is about perfection. For them, walking with God is solely about getting it right 100 percent of the time. No margin of error. No room for mistakes. Absolutely no room for weakness. These are the people who maintain the façade of holiness for so long that they're unable to recover when they're finally forced to deal with personal failure. Because they embrace the graceless life, when they desperately need grace they can't receive it. They've never come face-to-face with the grace of God! They knew the rules but not the God who longs for relationship. They know the 23rd Psalm, but they have never been intimate with the Shepherd about whom the psalm speaks.

Every new Christian begins his or her spiritual journey with the idea that "I am going to have a relationship with God." But so often, well-meaning disciples run out of spiritual fuel and find themselves not meeting their expectations of walking with God. Thus the question facing new Christians is "What does it mean to walk with God?"

Jeff is a new Christian who had a great start but now finds himself going through the motions and afraid to confide to anyone that he isn't sure anymore that God is real. He's troubled because, publicly, he confesses Christ but deep inside has many doubts about his faith.

Not long after his initial conversion, he noticed that some of the old habits he thought were behind him began to rise like suppressed sewage. How do you explain to your friends that some of the desires of your past sinful lifestyle have come back? How is it that one moment a person can feel so saved and the next minute be mired in a drab, dark dungeon of self-doubt? It seems that the pendulum of the soul swings easily from faith to feeling. How can this be?

No matter who we are, we're faced with some of the same rock-hard questions because walking with God is about transformation—which requires something to fade and something completely different to emerge.

TOUGH QUESTIONS ABOUT WALKING WITH GOD:

Think of me as a fellow-patient in the same hospital who, having been admitted a little earlier, could give some advice.—C.S. Lewis

Each time I ponder the words of C.S. Lewis, I'm forced to deal with the struggles I've faced while walking with God, and here's what I've found: In the areas where I'm strong, Satan often attacks me with pride. But in the places where I've failed, I have learned humility, and it's in those places where I have experienced the manifold grace of God. Thus, in the truest sense, we are indeed fellow patients or co-journeyers in a lifelong relationship with Jesus Christ, all the while learning (sometimes in the crucible of weakness) how to struggle, stumble, and finally stride confidently in our walk with the Savior.

At some point in the journey, most believers wonder why it is that in spite of their salvation experience, they still struggle with sinful desires. Is there a place where all our struggles will be over? Every believer will ultimately have at least one sin "that so easily trips us up" (Hebrews 12:1). The key to becoming victorious in our walk with God is to embrace the truth of God's Word that the "ruling power of sin" has been destroyed because of what Christ accomplished on the cross. The struggle with sin that happens in our human body can only be gradually disciplined by right choices until we are finally conformed to who we are in Jesus Christ. Romans offers some guidance:

From now on, think of it this way: Sin speaks a dead language that means nothing to you; God speaks your mother tongue, and you hang on every word. You are dead to sin and alive to God. That's what Jesus did. That means you must not give sin a vote in the way you conduct your lives. Don't give it the time of day (Romans 6:11-12—The Message).

My first year as a Christian was miserable, to tell the truth. I was plagued with unending doubts about my relationship with God. I wasn't sure if I was truly born again. I wondered whether I would go to heaven when I die. I spent many hours praying for God to give me a sign, some assurance that I was truly a Christian.

Looking back at that first year, I realize now that I was a victim of my insecurities. I wish I could tell you that at the end of that year of feeling like a failure, I had a powerful vision of God that incorporated angels ascending and descending. Alas, there was no trumpet, no strings, no clanging of cymbals.

What happened? I began to realize that my zeal for perfection hadn't originated with God but with my wayward insecurity. I was trying to be "good" so that I would earn God's love. Slowly but surely, I began to believe that God was a loving Father, not a Father waiting in heaven with a big eraser to remove my name from His book if I had a bad thought. I began to embrace the truth that I was God's child even on my worst day.

I remember the tears that flowed down my cheeks when it finally dawned on me that my salvation was secure not because of my performance but because Christ had paid the price with the blood He'd shed on the cross. It was a privilege to walk in relationship with this God who loved me before I even knew Him!

It cost God plenty to get you out of that dead-end, empty-headed life you grew up in. He paid with Christ's sacred blood, you know. He died like an unblemished, sacrificial lamb. And this was no afterthought. Even though it has only lately—at the end of the ages—become public knowledge, God always knew he was going to do this for you (1 Peter 1:18-20—The Message).

And I am certain that God, who began the good work within you, will continue his work until it is finally finished on the day when Christ returns (Philippians 1:6—NLT).

I know the one in whom I trust, and I am sure that he is able to guard what I have entrusted to him until the day of his return (2 Timothy 1:12—NLT).

So often in our walk with God we're quick to compare ourselves with others who seem to have it all together. Whenever we begin to compare, we fall prey to self-pity because most of the time we unconsciously focus on people who are worse off than we are. King David almost lost his spiritual balance because he began looking at wicked people who "seemed" to be prospering. Where is your focus? Are you looking at Christ?

John was the last of the original Band of Brothers, the men who went through nightmarish spiritual warfare together to establish the new Christian faith. The charismatic Peter had died for the Faith. The brilliant historian Luke was now dead. One by one, the news came that each had died the martyr's death. John's words are significant because he walked with God through many a valley and over steep hills. From the time he locked eyes with the carpenter from Nazareth, he never looked back. Here is what John wrote for all of us who dare to answer the call to walk with God:

If we claim we have no sin, we are only fooling ourselves and not living in the truth. But if we confess our sins to him, He is faithful and just to forgive us our sins and to cleanse us from all wickedness (1 John 1:8-9—NLT).

I believe that the Holy Spirit inspired John to write those words because God knows that, otherwise, we would wonder about the tension created as we attempt to live out our faith in real-life dramas. It's amid the maddening pace of life that we find ourselves feeling guilty about the times when we fail to keep up. Did God really intend for us to feel guilty if we missed praying for an hour each day? Or is He the kind of friend who loves you on the days when you talk for hours and loves you just as much on the days when you spend only five minutes? Is your relationship with God secure even during the long, weary days when you're a zombie because a newborn baby is keeping you up most of the night? Is it secure when you're caring for your elderly mother around the clock?

If you're in the "zombie season," you just might want to reflect on this passage: "So now there is no condemnation for those who belong to Christ Jesus. And because you belong to him, the power of the life-giving Spirit has freed you from the power of sin that lead to death" (Romans 12:1—NLT).

So there you have it. Walking with God isn't about being perfect. It isn't about following all the rules. If it were, it wouldn't be about God—it would be about your excellent report card.

The picture that God desires for us to see is one of relationship. Today, you are in a covenant relationship with the all-powerful, all knowing and all-wise God. There may be days when His presence is so overwhelming that you're awed by His nearness. And there may be other days when He seems to be light years away.

As you mature in your relationship with God, you grow into the realization that God is just as close on the days when you feel Him as He is on the days when the heavens seem to be nailed shut.

All things work for our good
Though sometimes we don't see how they could
Struggles that break our hearts in two
Sometimes blind us to the truth
Our Father knows what is best for us
His ways are not our own
So when your pathway grows dim
And you just don't see Him
Remember you're never alone

God is too wise to be mistaken
God is too good to be unkind
So when you don't understand
When you don't see His plan
When you can't trace His hand
Trust His heart

He sees the master plan
And He holds our future in His hand
So don't live as those who have no hope
All our hope is found in Him
We see the present clearly
But He sees the first and the last
And like a tapestry
He's weaving you and me
To someday be just like Him

A STEP ON THE JOURNEY:

How has your perception of God been aligned with how you were raised or with a flawed human relationship?

What verses of Scripture do you need to internalize so you can rewire faulty thinking?

❧ 8 ☙

THE LAND OF DRAGONS

(Wanted: Ordinary Heroes)

I didn't see any dragons here.
Plenty of snakes on the way over here, though.
—Oscar Wilde, *in* Here Be Dragons

If they longed for the country they came from, they could have
gone back. But they were looking for a better place
(Hebrews 11:15-16—NLT).

When Christopher Columbus set sail to find the New World, great uncertainty lay ahead. In the map's margins, the mapmakers had ominously written, "Here lie dragons and wild beasts." No one had ever been "here," and thus over time, legend had become reality and that false reality ruled with savage uncertainty. World explorers like Columbus knew that if they were going to make discoveries, they would have to have courage and step into the vast unknown and uncharted spaces of the world.

Walking with God isn't solely about certainty. It *involves* uncertainty—the people of the Bible whom we call "heroes" weren't certain of everything—but they acted on what they knew to be certain and they allowed God to take them to places they'd never been.

They were certain about God's character. They were certain about God's commitment to His Word. And they were certain about His power. Once those things were established, they allowed God to chart a course for their lives—a journey into the unknown.

We often hear the stories of great Christians like Martin Luther, John Wesley, John Wilberforce, Corrie Ten Boom and Dr. Martin Luther King, and deep down in our hearts we wonder if we have what they possessed. The fact of the matter is, they probably wondered the same thing about themselves. The difference between those who do and those who don't rarely has much to do with the traits we consider must-haves. In fact, the word used most often to describe the people we label "heroes" is *ordinary*.

Mary, the mother of Jesus, was simply ordinary—nothing about her would have set her apart from the thousands of virgin girls in her community. What made her special was the fact that God invited her to play a role in the revelation of his greatest gift to the world. *Ordinary* is the vessel into which God most often pours His greatest power. Consider the words of 1 Corinthians:

> *Take a good look, friends, at who you were when you got called into this life. I don't see many of the 'the brightest and the best' among you, not many influential, not many from high-society families. Isn't it obvious that God deliberately chose men and women that the culture overlooks and exploits and abuses, chose these 'nobodies' to expose the hallow pretensions of the 'somebodies' That makes it quite clear that*

none of you can get by with blowing your own horn before
God (1 Corinthians 1:26-29—The Message).

When we consider the varied characters of the Bible who
were instruments in the divine drama that began in the book
of Genesis and concludes in the book of Revelation, we quickly
understand that for all the things that were different about them,
one thing bound them together: None of them allowed their
relationship with God and, ultimately, their "divine assignment"
to go unfulfilled because they lacked the facts.

Walking with God isn't about having all the facts. Walking
with God isn't about scientific data that's been tested and
retested and been shown to be reliable. Walking with God isn't
about money-back guarantees, fail-safe formulas and maps.
Noah wasn't certain that the "big boat theory" would work. He
acted solely on the instructions that God had given him. His confidence was anchored in nothing more than the Word of a God
he had never seen, as shown in Hebrews: "By faith, Noah built
a ship in the middle of dry land. He was warned about something he couldn't see, and acted on what he was told" (Hebrews
11:7—The Message).

And Abraham had no map of the promised land. He walked
out of Ur of the Chaldees based simply on what God had told
him. "By an act of faith, Abraham said yes to God's call to travel
to an unknown place that would become his home. When he
left he had no idea where he was going" (Hebrews 11:8—The
Message).

Joseph was uncertain what would become of his dream. He
was thrown into a dark, damp pit, and God allowed him to
be sold as a slave to the household of Potiphar. God's blessing

upon Joseph's life spilled over, and the household of Potiphar was blessed because of Joseph.

But God wasn't finished. He also blessed Joseph by allowing the wife of Potiphar to accuse him of attempted rape. Joseph's next stop on his walk with God wasn't the comfort of the Ritz-Carlton but a filthy jail cell, and it was here that his character formation shines brightly. Most of us would have landed in prison, bitten by the venom of bitterness. If I'd been Joseph, this would have been a great time to declare, "I don't do dreams." After all, it had been a dream that started his downward slide. But ultimately, the dreamer arrived at the house of the Pharaoh! Joseph traded in the prison robe for the Prime Minister's robe. Here's the progression:

+ *His brothers rip the coat of many colors from his back.*

+ *"Mrs. Potiphar" grabs his second coat.*

+ *He receives a coat upon his arrival in prison.*

+ *The Pharaoh removes the prison coat and replaces it with the Prime Minister's coat!*

The journey that God chose for Joseph serves as a powerful metaphor for the person who's walking in a difficult place without the knowledge of how the narrative will play out. Just because God hasn't shown you everything doesn't mean that you've missed God's will. It took over thirty years of uncertainty before these verses could be written: "And Joseph remembered the dreams he'd dreamed about them many years before" (Genesis 42:9—NLT).

And these: "Don't you see, you planned evil against me but God used those same plans for my good, as you see all around you right now—life for many people" (Genesis 50:20—The Message).

Walking with God and uncertainty go hand in hand. If you have any doubts, just ask Matthew. He was as the "numbers guy" among the twelve disciples Jesus chose. Everything had to be exact. Every dollar had to be accounted for. For tax collectors, it all came down to calculating the numbers—nothing was left to feelings or faith. Just show him the numbers and Matthew was in his comfort zone.

And then everything changed. He was sitting in the tax office when "the carpenter" came calling and, with him, great uncertainty. When Jesus' eyes locked on to his and He said, "Come follow me," Matthew decided to walk away from a lucrative business and set out to discover the unknowns of "the road less traveled."

In Matthew 11, he shares the following story:

> When Jesus had finished giving these instructions to his twelve disciples, he went out to teach and preach in towns throughout the region. John the Baptist, who was in prison, heard about all the things the Messiah was doing. So he sent his disciples to ask Jesus, "Are you the Messiah we've been expecting, or should we keep looking for someone else?" Jesus told them, "Go back to John and tell him what you have heard and seen—the blind see, the lame walk, the lepers are cured, the deaf hear, the dead are raised to life, and the Good News is being preached to the poor (Matthew 11:1-5—NLT).

At that moment, I imagine, Jesus employed one of his "pregnant pauses." Just enough time for everyone—especially Mr. Numbers—to realize that He had no plans to break John out of prison. As that dreadful thought started to sink in, Jesus continued, "Blessed is he who does not take offense at me" (Matthew 11:6—NASB).

What was He saying? There's a special blessing for us when we refuse to allow the tension caused by our uncertainty to cause us to become "offended" by God.

No sooner had John's disciples left to convey to him Jesus' strange words than the Lord gave John the greatest compliment possible: "Let me tell you what's going on here: No one in history surpasses John the Baptizer" (Matthew 11:11—The Message). I just wish John could have heard it!

From what we know of history, though, John didn't need to hear it. When the time came, he walked into the death chamber and surrendered his head. How did he do it? When you've surrendered your heart to Christ, nothing else matters. Nothing can be taken from you. When Christ has your heart, He has all of you.

Walking with God is about surrender. Paul implored the Christians in Rome to "present your bodies a living sacrifice" (Romans 12:1-2). The natural instinct is to move only when everything is guaranteed, but this is not the life that God has called us to. Walking with God is about losing your life. It is about dying to self. It is about forsaking mother and father. It is about walking by faith and not by sight.

When Columbus set sail, there were those who doubted that he would come back. They believed that the maps were correct; at the edge of the "known" was the place of dragons. But Columbus refused to believe the "experts." He believed that the maps were wrong; the world wasn't flat. And ultimately, he sailed beyond the maps and changed history. Sometimes in walking with God, you have to lay everything on the line and trust the still, small voice of the Spirit. You simply set the sails of your soul, catch the wind of the Holy Spirit and allow Him to lead you. As John put it:

The wind blows where it wishes, and you hear the sound of it, but cannot tell where it comes from and where it goes. So is everyone who is born of the Spirit (John 3:8—NKJV).

> *But to every mind there openeth,*
> *A way, and way, and away,*
> *A high soul climbs the highway,*
> *And the low soul gropes the low,*
> *And in between on the misty flats,*
> *The rest drift to and fro.*

> *But to every man there openeth,*
> *A high way and a low,*
> *And every mind decideth,*
> *The way his soul shall go.*

> *One ship sails East,*
> *And another West,*
> *By the self-same winds that blow,*
> *'Tis the set of the sails*
> *And not the gales,*
> *That tells the way we go.*

> *Like the winds of the sea*
> *Are the waves of time,*
> *As we journey along through life,*
> *'Tis the set of the soul,*
> *That determines the goal,*
> *And not the calm or the strife*

—Ella Wheeler Wilcox

During my years of walking with God, I've noticed that the people who are fearful of walking with God outside their comfort zones often spend their days in their comfortable place inventing mythical "dragons" that become larger and larger as time passes.

What lie have you allowed to anchor you to your past? What lie has Satan whispered into your mind that has kept you caged? You hold the key. You're free only when you embrace God's truth. As John said, "Then you will know the truth, and the truth will set you free" (John 8:32—NIV).

When Columbus returned, the coins of Spain were re-minted. The old inscription, "No more beyond," was replaced with "More beyond!" God's challenge to you and me is to deal with the "dragons" just as Columbus did. You might be dealing with fear, regret, a failed marriage, or an addiction—whatever the dragon, focus your vision on Jesus Christ and move in spite of uncertainty. More Beyond!

A STEP ON THE JOURNEY:

Defeating the Dragons:

FEAR: "For God has not given us a spirit of fear and timidity, but of power, love and self-discipline" (2 Timothy 1:7—NLT).

LOW SELF-ESTEEM: "For we are God's masterpiece. He has created us anew in Christ Jesus, so we can do the good things he planned for us long ago" (Ephesians 2:10—NLT).

ADDICTION: "The Spirit of the LORD is upon me, for he has anointed me to bring Good News to the poor. He has sent me to proclaim that captives will be released" (Luke 4:19—NLT).

SPIRITUAL EXHAUSTION: *"Come to me, all of you who are weary and carry heavy burdens, I will give you rest. Take my yoke upon you. Let me teach you...and you will find rest for your souls. For my yoke is easy to bear, and the burden I give you is light"* (Matthew 11:28-30—NLT).

9

FINDING PEACE OVER LAKE MICHIGAN

(ENCOUNTERING CHRIST IN A CRISIS)

It was a clear and crisp Chicago morning, nothing out of the ordinary, but sometimes ordinary can be deceiving. Sometimes, just on the other side of ordinary is a divine drama waiting to unfold.

I wasn't thinking about eternity. I was simply enjoying a smooth flight out of Chicago and looking forward to an uneventful trip back to Sacramento, California. But God had other plans.

It was just a few minutes into the flight. My eyes were closed, and my wife was beside me, already asleep, when I heard what sounded like a small explosion. The man sitting across the aisle from me yelled at the top of his lungs. "We've just lost power in one engine. We have to make an emergency landing." At that moment, I wanted to strangle him. I'd wanted to break the news to my wife without any drama, but now fear had to be managed. I'd never been in an emergency situation on a flight, and I'd often wondered what a moment like this would be like—the moment when you realize that God and life's circumstances have placed you in a position where you are absolutely not in control. If ever I needed peace, I needed it at that moment.

The air was thick with panic. Grown men wept visibly. Mothers clutched children. My wife and I, along with others, prayed aloud as the plane circled over Lake Michigan while dumping the fuel in preparation for the emergency landing. It seemed like an eternity.

Was this how my walk with God would end? How would our families cope with our loss? I told Marion how much I loved her and we held hands. The only comfort we had in that moment was in the fact that we were ending our walk with God together.

When we began the descent, I prayed with my wife one last time. We bowed our heads. The ground rose to meet the plane ...

And then the plane touched down. Safely. Everyone cheered. On the way out, we hugged the flight attendants and the pilots. And I thought about what had happened inside me only minutes before, when panic could have replaced peace. But more about that in a moment.

So often we sing about God's peace and we hear preaching about peace, but let's face it—we often find ourselves lacking this elusive thing called peace. This was as true for those who first walked with Jesus as it is for us today.

One of my favorite passages is found the Gospel of Luke 24. It's the story of two disciples walking down the road from the city of Emmaus. Despite the many times Jesus had told His followers about his crucifixion, they were simply not prepared. They weren't prepared to see Him beaten mercilessly. They weren't prepared to see Him hanging from the cross with a crown of thorns on His head. They weren't prepared for the thought that He would no longer be with them. They had no peace.

The post-resurrection story is a powerful reminder that walking with God means nothing if we're lacking in peace. Here's how Luke recounts the story:

*That same day two of Jesus' followers were walking to the
village of Emmaus, seven miles from Jerusalem. As they walked
along they were talking about everything that had happened.
As they talked and discussed these things, Jesus himself suddenly came and began walking with them. But God kept them
from recognizing him (Luke 24:13-16—NLT).*

Just imagine the fear that must have captivated the hearts of
these men as they walked the longest seven miles of their lives.
They were "dead men walking" because they had no hope.
Hopelessness prevented them from recognizing the stranger who
joined them at some point along the journey. Mile after long mile,
they walked with their eyes closed and their hearts heavy.

Here's how it ended:

*By the time they were nearing Emmaus and the end of their
journey, Jesus acted as if he were going on, but they begged
him, "stay the night with us, since it is getting late." So he
went home with them. As they sat down to eat, he took the
bread and blessed it. The he broke it and gave it to them.
Suddenly, their eyes were opened, and they recognized him.
And at that moment he disappeared (Luke 24:28-31—NLT).*

The Risen Christ had been walking and talking with them,
but their anxiety and grief prevented them seeing Him. Does that
sound familiar? Are you allowing a situation that seems hopeless
to rob you of the peace that Jesus Christ is offering? Are you
walking down a lonely, depressed path contemplating the "best"
way to end your life? Are you just going through the motions each
Sunday at church, having lost the reality of intimacy with God?

The truth that we must embrace in the darkest moments,
when we're crippled by fear, is that the Holy Spirit is with us.

Before He ascended to heaven, Jesus said, "I am leaving you with a gift—peace of mind and heart. And the peace I give is a gift the world cannot give. So don't be troubled or afraid" (John 14:27—NLT). That's what Jesus had for these two defeated disciples and that's what He has for you.

When the two disciples sat with the stranger for the evening meal, they invited him to bless it. As He began to pray, something was awakened in their hearts. His was the same voice that had boldly called Lazarus back from the place of the dead. It was the voice that had commanded the demons to depart from the frail, broken body of a young child. They knew this voice. They had heard Him speak in the middle of a storm. They could still hear Him say, "Peace be still" (Mark 4:39—NKJV). Everything was beginning to make sense—all the times He had told them He would be crucified and, three days later, resurrected.

> They said to each other, "Didn't our hearts burn within us as he talked with us on the road and explained the scriptures to us?" (v. 32)

My biggest surprise that eventful morning over Chicago was the fact that I achieved peace. It reminded me that the Holy Spirit who lives in me is my source of comfort for every situation I face.

Here's what I now know about peace since that harrowing morning over Chicago:

+ *Peace comes only in the moments when we realize that what we're facing is out of our control.*

+ *Peace comes when we realize that God is the ultimate commander of our lives.*

+ *Peace comes when we understand that God is the "author and finisher" of our faith (Hebrews 12.1-2). The fact is, I cannot die until the last chapter of my God-ordained story has been completed. As Philippians 1:23 says, "God who started a good work in you and me has committed to finishing it."*

+ *Peace comes when I have an intimate relationship with the Holy Spirit, which Jesus called "the comforter," or the paracletos (someone who walks with you).*

PRAYER:

Jesus, today I choose to walk in Your peace. I confess that You are the Lord of every situation that I will face. No matter what happens, I know that You hold my world in the palm of Your hands. Fear is an impostor. I refuse to open the door for fear. Today I chose to allow the peace of God to guard my mind. In Jesus' name I pray. Amen.

A STEP ON THE JOURNEY:

And the peace of God, which surpasses all understanding, will guard your hearts and minds through Christ Jesus (Philippians 4:7—NKJV).

And let the peace of God rule in your hearts, to which also you were called in one body; and be thankful (Colossians 3:15—NKJV).

Make a list of decisions, challenges or fears that you will ask God to help you with by granting you His peace.

⇒ 10 ⇐

KEEP ON
KEEPING ON

(The Power of Consistency)

I thank God through Jesus for every one of you. That's first.
People everywhere keep telling me about your lives of faith, and every
time I hear them, I thank him (Romans 1:8—The Message).

Toward the end of World War II, a B-17 Flying Fortress was flying a bombing raid over Germany when it was rocked by a sudden jolt. The bomber had taken a direct hit from enemy anti-aircraft guns on the ground, and the crew braced for the worst: a sudden burst of flames, followed quickly by death.

But in his book *The Fall of the Fortress*, Elmer Bendiner recounts how, even though several of the shells pierced the fuel tank, the plane was able to land without breaking apart or exploding in the air.

When an inspection was conducted, it was discovered that several of the twenty-millimeter shells remained intact, still embedded in the fuselage. Why hadn't these shells exploded? After they were carefully removed, the mystery was solved: they were empty. There were no explosives inside. How could this have happened?

The final mystery was solved when, upon opening one of the shells, a handwritten note was found, written in the Czech language. "This is all we can do for now," it read. A courageous freedom fighter in the Czech underground had infiltrated a German munitions factory and made sure the shells were produced without explosives.

In his book *Simple Faith*, author Chuck Swindoll commented on the story:

> *That same person may have died wondering if the quiet work he was doing to subvert the enemy war machine would ever make any difference to the outcome of the war. Nevertheless he pressed on, doing what little he could each day, letting the future take care of itself ... and indeed it did. There was a Flying Fortress crew who had him to thank for their lives and their future.* [4]

Imagine the tension that must have been a part of the lives of these Czech underground fighters. At any second they could have been discovered and put to death. Each day they dug deep and found a reservoir of courage and faith that allowed them to act without knowing how things would end. Every day they wondered, "Are we making a difference?" Every day they showed up believing they were.

Walking with God is about faith, but faith isn't passive. Faith is never easy. Faith can also be spelled R-I-S-K. Walking with God is a "faith walk" because many are the moments when you don't know the full impact of what you're doing. Quite often we think we're walking with God just for ourselves, but the truth is that we walk with God not just for ourselves but for others. Faith has always been the difference-maker!

Recently, I've begun reflecting on the impact of my godly mother. The years of walking with God have taken their toll. She still has the same slender frame I've always known, but now she walks slower. Watching her reminds me of the humorist Erma Bombeck's observation about the passing of time and her relationship with her aging mother: "The mother has become the daughter and the daughter has become the mother."

Similarly, I see that I have become the father and Mom has become my little girl. Yet I remain amazed at her consistency and dedication to walking with God. It would take fifty years of prayer before my dad fully committed his heart to Christ, but Mom kept on keeping on. She is fiercely committed to God's kingdom. When we moved to New York in 1971, her first priority was to make sure her children had a church to attend. A few years later, when a young pastor in that congregation decided to plant a new church, Mom volunteered to help him.

That first Sunday was scary. There we were, the pastor and his wife and their two young children. And then there was my mom with her seven boys.

Later, when the small struggling congregation needed money to renovate the rented building, Mom went to the bank, borrowed the money and gave it to the church. She then made the payments until the loan was repaid in full.

At the great age of 77, Mom is now something of a legend. Young mothers ask her to pray over them so that they will be able to raise their children to be great Christians. Everywhere she goes, people who have known her refer to her as "the lady with the seven boys." Each Sunday, several thousand people attend the churches that five of her sons pastor in New York, northern Virginia and Atlanta.

What was her secret? There were several, actually:

+ *She understood the power of doing the right thing over a long period of time.*

+ *She believed that by placing God's kingdom first, she would reap the reward later.*

+ *She refused to place a "time limit" on her prayers.*

+ *She infected her children with her passion for God's church.*

+ *She continued to pray even when it seemed her prayers bore no fruit.*

+ *She challenged her sons to give their lives to Christian service and influenced several generations of mothers to dream big dreams for their sons and daughters.*

Walking with God means remaining faithful to your calling even when you're unaware of what the results will be. Many a Christian will stand before the *bema,* or the judgment seat, and be surprised at the rewards they will receive (2 Corinthians 5:10). We don't always know what is transpiring in the invisible realm—it's only in the afterlife that you will fully understand the power of your continued prayers. The time spent on your knees each day affects more than you see, more than you know, and more than you can imagine.

Your service to the local church cannot be measured in dollars and cents. When we stand before God and the books are opened, only then will you fully appreciate the fact that your service allowed untold numbers of people to be reached for Christ. As 1 Corinthians says:

So my dear brothers and sisters, be strong and immovable. Always work enthusiastically for the Lord, for you know that nothing you do for the Lord is ever useless (1 Corinthians 15:58—NLT).

The King James translators used the word *steadfast*. The word connotes the idea of strong steel girders like those that hold up the Golden Gate Bridge. They weather sun and rain, and when the cold damp fog rolls in, they remain. They have remained steadfast.

Here's how Dr. Earl Palmer, who pastored the First Presbyterian Church of Berkeley, described the bridge:

> *I have often thought of the Golden Gate Bridge in San Francisco as our city's boldest structure in that its great south pier rests directly upon the fault zone of the San Andreas Fault. That bridge is an amazing structure of both flexibility and strength. It is built to sway some twenty feet at the center of its one-mile suspension span. The secret to its durability is its flexibility that enables the sway, but that is not all. By design, every part of the bridge—its concrete roadway, its steel railings, its cross beams—is inevitably related from one welded joint to the other up through the vast cable system to two great towers and two great land anchor piers. The towers bear most of the weight, and they are deeply embedded into the rock foundation beneath the sea. In other words, the bridge is totally preoccupied with its foundation. This is its secret! Flexibility and foundation.*[5]

The Scriptures speak to the issue of flexibility and foundation. Consider:

FLEXIBILITY:

> *What then is my pay? It is the opportunity to preach the Good News without charging anyone. That's why I never demand my rights when I preach the Good News. Even though I am a free man with no master, I have become a slave to all people to bring many to Christ. When I was with the Jews, I lived*

like a Jew to bring the Jews to Christ. When I was with those who follow the Jewish law, I too lived under that law. Even though I am not subject to the law, I did this so I could bring to Christ those who are under the law.

When I am with the Gentiles who do not follow the Jewish law, I too live apart from the law so I can bring them to Christ. But I do not ignore the law of God; I obey the law of Christ.

When I am with those who are weak, I share their weakness, for I want to bring the weak to Christ. Yes, I try to find common ground with everyone, doing everything I can to save some (1 Corinthians 9:18-22—NLT).

FOUNDATION:

He shall be like a tree planted by the rivers of water, that brings forth fruit in its season, whose leaf also shall not wither; and whatever he does shall prosper (Psalm 1:3—NKJV).

When we stand before the judgment seat, I'll be hoping to catch a glimpse of some of the courageous Czech freedom fighters. I want to see the expression on their faces when our Heavenly Father calls out the names of the many soldiers who were saved by their act of courage—saved because the freedom fighters kept on keeping on.

P.S. I expect to see you there, too!

A STEP ON THE JOURNEY:

Take a moment and make a list of four people who are sources of inspiration to you. Take the time to send them a note and thank them for their faith.

⇒ 11 ⇐

THE UNKNOWN REBEL

(We Were Chosen To Make a Difference)

Through acts of faith, they toppled kingdoms, made justice work, took the promises for themselves (Hebrews 11:33—The Message).

In April 1998, *Time* magazine included "The Unknown Rebel" in the feature "Time 100: The Most Important People of the Century"[6]:

The incident took place near Tiananmen on Chang'an Avenue, which runs east-west along the south end of the Forbidden City in Beijing. It was June 5, 1989, one day after the Chinese government's violent crackdown on the Tiananmen protests.

The man placed himself alone in the middle of the street as the tanks approached. He was now directly in the path of the armored vehicle. Observers noted that he held two shopping bags, one in each hand. The tanks came to a stop. The man gestured toward the tanks with his bags. In response, the lead tank attempted to drive around the man, but the man repeatedly stepped into the path of the tank in a show of nonviolent action. After repeatedly attempting to go around, rather than crush the man, the lead tank stopped its engines, and the armored vehicles behind it seemed to follow suit. There was a short pause, with the man and the tanks having reached a quiet, still impasse.

Having successfully brought the column to a halt, the man climbed onto the hull of the buttoned-up lead tank and, after briefly stopping at the driver's hatch, he appeared in video footage of the incident to call into various ports in the tank's turret. He then climbed atop the turret and seemed to have a short conversation with a crew member at the gunner's hatch. After ending the conversation, the man alighted from the tank. The tank commander briefly emerged from his hatch, and the tanks restarted their engines, ready to continue on. At that point, the man, who was still standing within a meter or two from the side of the lead tank, leapt in front of the vehicle once again and quickly reestablished the man-versus-tank standoff.

Video footage from that day's bizarre encounter showed that two figures in blue attire then pulled the man away and disappeared with him into a nearby crowd. At that point, the tanks continued on their way.

Eyewitnesses disagree about the identity of the people who pulled him aside.

It's a strange thing about the truly great moments. They seem so embryonic and then they mushroom. They take on a larger-than-life significance that lives on long after the thought that precipitated the initial action. They're like the minute atom, so small. They seem mundane, but when activated, they explode.

Why? Because inside every small atom is an explosion waiting to be ignited. Atomic!

We do not walk with God in and through large blocks of time. We walk with Him in minute moments. We're too quick to count years and decades and centuries while ignoring the moments. The seemingly insignificant fragments of time that, when added to another and another over time, create a decisive moment and help to shape human history.

Quite often in walking with God, there are moments that present us with an opportunity to act or to speak. Why do we miss them so often? Because we're prone to thinking of a big God and big challenges but an insignificant "me." And it's true—compared with the God who made trillions of stars, we are small. It's true that the creative force that stretched out the planets and keeps the universe in order with the sound of his voice is huge and we are small. In Psalm 8, the author addresses this issue:

God, brilliant Lord, yours is a household name.
Nursing infants gurgle choruses about you;
Toddlers shout the songs
That drown out enemy talk,
and silence atheist babble.
I look up at your macro-skies, dark and enormous,
Your handmade sky-jewelry,
Moon and stars mounted in their settings.
Then I look at my micro-self and wonder,
Why do you bother with us?
Why take a second look our way?
Yet we've so narrowly missed being gods,
Bright with Eden's dawn light.
You put us in charge of your handcrafted world,
Repeated to us your Genesis-charge,

Made us lords of sheep and cattle,
Even animals out in the wild,
Birds flying and fish swimming,
Whales singing in the ocean deeps.
God, brilliant Lord,
Your name echoes around the world.

Picture the "unknown rebel" again. A huge drama was playing out on the world stage, thanks to the power of the media. The cast included the mighty military machine of the Communist government of China and the courage of people whose names we'll probably never know, many of whom would be murdered or maimed. Some would be arrested and others would be plucked from their homes under the murky shadow of night, never to be heard from again. The rebel appeared from out of nowhere, rather like a party-crasher. He didn't belong there. Who stands in front of an approaching column of tanks? Who dares to pit 150 pounds against tons of steel? One man did. The world watched and millions were inspired.

Walking with God is often about being prepared for moments when you must stand in the face of adversity. Though you know that by yourself you're no match for the opposition, you stand anyway. It's standing because not to stand would be to acknowledge that you are powerless. You are not powerless—the invisible God of the universe stands with you. An "innumerable company of angels" stands around you.

The angel of the LORD encamps all around those who fear
Him, And delivers them (Psalm 34:7—NKJV).

There is a tension that exists in the Christian faith. On one hand, we understand the danger of pride. As James says, "God resists the proud but gives grace to the humble" (James 4:6). The picture created by the Greek word **resists (antitassomai)** is that of a mighty general who has vowed to engage in a timeless struggle to crush the opposing force. This verse and others are reminders that God hates pride. It was pride that brought revolution to heaven. It was pride that caused one-third of heaven's angelic force to array themselves with the "Sun of the Morning" against their creator. Pride produced hell!

On the other hand, to walk with God we must understand who we are in Christ, and that's where the tension is created. The Scriptures speak to the fact that we are overcomers. We are more than conquerors. Romans says:

> *Who shall separate us from the love of Christ? Shall tribulation, or distress, or persecution, or famine, or nakedness, or peril, or sword? As it is written: "For Your sake we are killed all day long; We are accounted as sheep for the slaughter." Yet in all these things we are more than conquerors through Him who loved us (Romans 8:35-37—NKJV).*

A careful reading of the creation story leads us to believe that when God created Adam and Eve in the Garden of Eden, they were created not only *by* God but also *for* God. Man was created to govern the garden under God's authority. Adam was not weak. He was not timid. He was not unsure of his place and position in the Garden. When he walked hand in hand with Eve, every creature watched them and understood that they had been created in the "image" and "likeness" of God.

Satan was able to destroy God's government in the Garden of Eden by corrupting Adam and Eve's vision of God and ultimately their understanding of who they were. Walking with God demands an understanding of who you are in Christ. Refuse to be defined by your bank account, your possessions, your failures, or your feelings. You are God's Child. You can do what God says you can do. Nothing is impossible if God is on your side.

What impossible situation are you currently facing? Walking with God is about realizing that God wants you to win in this moment. God desires to give you the courage and the strength to deal with the "tanks" attempting to intimidate you.

The fact that you were raised in a dysfunctional environment is not the final word on who you are. You have the courage to face down your past and live in the joy of wholesome relationships. The fact that you were fired from your last job can become the defining voice in your life if you allow it. Instead, you could choose to erase the negative messages and record new and powerful messages from God's Word:

+ *I have strength for any challenge that comes my way (Psalm 121).*

+ *I am a new person because of my faith in Christ (2 Corinthians 5:17).*

+ *My sins have been removed from God's book (Colossians 2:11-32).*

+ *I am destined for success and not failure (Revelation 5:8-10).*

You are not the weakling that your adversary would have you believe. This moment is right for you to do something that may seem totally impossible. Today you could begin praying that God will turn a difficult situation around. Today you could find the courage to face a problem you had hoped would go away. Today you could begin embracing the "new creation" that God declares that you are. Today you could step onto a stage where you seemingly don't belong. When you do, the power of God can be unleashed from inside you. Remember, inside the small atom is the possibility of an explosion!

> *For though we walk in the flesh, we do not war according to the flesh, for the weapons of our warfare are not of the flesh, but divinely powerful for the destruction of fortresses. We are destroying speculations and every lofty thing raised up against the knowledge of God, and we are taking every thought captive to the obedience of Christ (2 Corinthians 10:3-5—NASB).*

A STEP ON THE JOURNEY:

Take the next seven days to reprogram your mind with the Word of God and begin the process of being morphed into the person God meant for you to be.

Monday. I have the strength of Christ *(2 Corinthians 12:9-10).*
Tuesday: I am a new person in Christ *(2 Corinthians 5:17).*
Wednesday: I have God's Wisdom *(James 1:5).*
Thursday: I have God's Peace *(John 14:27).*
Friday: I have the authority to use God's name *(John 14:13-14).*
Saturday: I have access to God *(Hebrews 4:16).*
Sunday: I have the Holy Spirit to teach me *(John 14:26).*

~ 12 ~

INFLUENCE WITH GOD

(PRAYER: THE MOST POWERFUL FORCE IN THE UNIVERSE)

Something must be wrong. Maybe I don't have enough faith. I pray, but it seems that my prayers are rarely answered. I've stopped expecting anything to happen.

I prayed at the start of the relationship. I didn't want to be hurt again. I thought for sure I had found the right person. I was wrong. I don't understand why God allowed me to get hurt, ... to make another mistake. Does God really care?

The doctor walked into the room and told me I had breast cancer. I didn't know how to act and so I just stared at him. That was the moment I gave up. I just knew I was going to die.

Walking with God doesn't imply powerlessness in the face of circumstances. In heaven, we will look back and realize the many situations that we could have influenced with our prayers if we hadn't become distracted. We lost our focus and ended up being routed in the battles that should have been won.

You may be facing something that seems out of control, but the truth is that you have more influence with God than you think.

Abraham left the city of Ur without any reservations. He was convinced that God—the invisible God of the universe—had called him to walk away from everything and take the journey to a place he didn't know (Genesis 12:1). Among the family members who accompanied him was his ambitious nephew Lot. The short stocky body, the distinct nose, and the darting eyes painted a portrait of someone who was insecure, quick-tempered, and hasty in his decisions, and these traits combined to make Lot a prime candidate for Satan's cunning devices.

Ultimately, success went to immature Lot's head. He became a different person. He and Abraham had prospered in a short period of time, and Lot believed their success was due to his abilities. The land wasn't big enough for the both of them.

Negotiations broke down. Harsh words were exchanged. They parted ways at the suggestion of Abraham. The last time Abraham saw him, Lot was arrogantly headed toward the twin cities of Sodom and Gomorrah.

In Genesis 18, three angels are headed to destroy Sodom and Gomorrah, and God decides to bring His "covenant partner" in on what's about to transpire:

> *Shall I hide from Abraham what I am doing, since Abraham shall surely become a great and mighty nation, and all the nations of the earth shall be blessed in him? For I have known him, in order that he may command his children and his household after him, that they keep the way of the LORD, to do righteousness and justice that the LORD may bring to Abraham what He has spoken to him (Genesis 18:17-19—NKJV).*

When he found out that God was about to unleash his judgment, "Abraham stood before the Lord" (Genesis 18:22—NKJV).

The scene evokes the image of a four-year-old under the watchful eye of his father, unaware of the force of nature. He runs along the shoreline of a white sandy beach attempting to keep the powerful waves from washing up on shore. Or picture ourselves, trying in vain to hold back the aging process with creams and expensive surgeries. Imagine someone trying to stop the Earth from spinning on its axis and you get the idea. Standing before God, Abraham seemed to be attempting the impossible.

Imagine the entire Angelic host peering over the balconies of heaven. Everything in the creation paused to witness one lonely Bedouin bargaining with the God of the universe. It had never been done! Never had there been such a prayer meeting! How long did it last? No one knows. What we do know is that in the end it seemed as if God had allowed Abraham to prevail. Abraham was his friend. He understood God because they had walked together.

The premise was that God would not destroy the righteous with the unrighteous. They opened negotiations at 50 lives:

God said, "If I find fifty decent people in the city of Sodom, I'll spare the place just for them." Abraham came back, "Do I, a mere mortal made from a handful of dirt, dare open my mouth again to my Master? What if the fifty fall short by five—would you destroy the city because of those missing five?" He said, "I won't destroy it if there are forty-five." Abraham spoke up again, "What if you only find forty?" "Neither will I destroy it if for forty." He said, "Master, don't be irritated with me, but what if only thirty are found?" "No, I won't do it if I find thirty." He pushed on, "I know I'm trying your patience, Master, but how about for twenty?" "I won't destroy it for twenty." He wouldn't quit, "Don't get angry, Master—this is the last time. What if you only come up with ten?" "For the sake of only ten, I won't destroy the city." When God finished talking with Abraham, he left. And Abraham went home (Genesis 18:26-33—The Message).

We all know what it feels like to watch circumstances veer out of our control. Despite our persuasive powers, we often find ourselves at the end of reason. We desperately grasp at straws, trying to find a handle to the unreachable places within someone's heart. We've all experienced that sinking feeling when we see something and those we love do not; they simply refuse to deal with the glaring light of reality. In spite of your best efforts, you realize that the snake of false success is seducing someone you love. How do you respond?

The early years of your marriage were about getting ahead and providing for the family. You both worked hard, and in the years that followed you were able to afford the nice home, the nice car, vacations, and so on. God did his part, but it seemed that somewhere along the line the desire to have more became an insatiable monster.

At first you wondered if there was another woman or man, but that was soon ruled out. It wasn't someone else but some*thing* else. You might have preferred that it *had* been an affair—at least then your competition would have had a face you could confront. There was no face, there was no person to battle against, but the deception was nonetheless real.

Is there anything you can do? Yes!

Abraham is a reminder that when we pray, we can influence God. In heaven we will look back at our journey with God through the moments of our lives and we will fully understand that our prayers moved the hand and the heart of God. And we will see the many moments when things could have been different if we had stood our ground in prayer. The fact is, we're too intimidated by the "big circumstances" of life.

There's the life we live and the life that we should have lived. There's the story that unfolded with the unfinished chapter. The hero didn't arrive in time. The mission failed. But there's another story—your story. The one that God wrote long before time began. A marriage was saved. A prodigal returned home. Grace covered a sin. Faith made the difference. Death didn't have the last word.

Prayer was the key.

Never stop praying (1 Thessalonians 5:17—NLT).

A STEP ON THE JOURNEY:

Begin a new journey with God in prayer by making use of a prayer journal.

Each day, clearly write a note to God asking him to assist you. The key is to be specific. At the end of the prayer, indicate the date you made the request, and when it's answered, indicate that date, too.

The goal is to have a catalog of prayers—some answered, some unanswered, but each one prayed with faith and expectancy.

$\leadsto$ 13 $\leadsto$

THE MISSION IS POSSIBLE

(You Matter More to God Than You Think)

We look upon prayer as a means for getting something for ourselves.
Pray that we may get to know God himself.
—Oswald Chambers

There is a real sense that your home has become a war zone. Day after day, the fighting is fierce! The injuries keep mounting like in the stories coming out of Afghanistan or some war-weary battle zone. The attacker isn't a stranger, though. That would have been easier. No, the attacker is your daughter. Something has gone terribly awry. The personality that was once serene and easy to love has changed, at first gradually and now rapidly.

You're emotionally spent. The arguments, the savage insults and the lies have all taken their toll. You wonder when you stopped being a great mom. You've morphed into a combative warrior who has to stand toe to toe with a teenage terrorist—a disturbed girl who views her mother as public enemy No. 1.

Is there anything you can do? Yes!

In the previous chapter, we saw Abraham wield the mighty weapon of prayer. God had informed Abraham of his intent to destroy the cities of Sodom and Gomorrah, and he stood before God on behalf of his nephew Lot—bound for those very cities. I've often wondered why God even bothered to tell Abraham. He was God. He could have done whatever He wanted. It seems that God was bound by his covenant relationship with Abraham. God wanted to tell Abraham because he *knew* that Abraham would appeal to his sense of justice. He knew that Abraham would pray.

God longs for us to ask Him to do the seemingly impossible.

You've been involved in your church for almost as long as you can remember. At the start, you were excited to serve. You were the male version of Mary in the New Testament. You were fulfilled in the kitchen while the "Martha" people enjoyed the "spiritual stuff." The fuel that kept you going was the fact that the more you "did," the more indispensable you felt. In a sense, they needed you and you needed them to *continue* needing you. The narcotic of being needed gave you a rush. It made you feel *significant.*

All that began to change. It didn't happen in a day or a week. It happened so slowly that you didn't see it coming. Your wife began to resent the fact that you were "just the church cook who lives with me and sleeps in the same bed." Eventually, she became angry at the church, and by the time she quit attending church, she was angry with God.

In the middle of your despair, is there anything you can do? Again, the answer is yes. Prayer influences the God who controls circumstances.

From an early age, you made the commitment to become a godly man. Years later, you married your sweetheart with the dream of "happily ever after." There was just one problem: She didn't share your passion for Christian service. In fact, she has become resentful of your "endless church talk." Recently, she admitted that she was never really a Christian.

For this situation and all others, God invites us to come to Him believing in the power of our prayers. Abraham's intense intercessory prayer session is a reminder of what can transpire in our walk with God. Make no mistake—walking with God is not a leisurely stroll through the garden of life. Walking with God will involve those moments when we find ourselves facing the giant—the seemingly towering challenges that are so overwhelming. They try to intimidate us into doing nothing.

Sometimes we walk with God while waging a fierce spiritual battle over a marriage that seems headed for divorce, a daughter who seems to be caught in the grip of Satan, or a sickness that seems intent on stealing someone whom you love. Fortunately, we've been given the most powerful force in the universe: prayer. The disciples could have asked for many things. They could have asked for the ability to speak or the ability to call down fire. But none of these mattered. They asked: "Teach us to pray" (Luke 11:1).

A final word, Be strong in the Lord and in his might power. Put on all God's armor so that you will be able to stand firm against all strategies of the devil. For we are not fighting against flesh-and-blood enemies. But against evil rulers and authorities of the unseen world, against mighty powers in this dark world, and against evil sprits in heavenly places. Therefore, put on every piece of God's armor so you will be able to resist the enemy in the time of evil. Then after the battle you will still be standing firm. Stand your ground (Ephesians 6:10-14—NLT).

This is what Abraham did. He stood his ground in prayer. And this is what you can do. Walking with God involves praying desperate prayers. James called them "effectual fervent prayers" (James 5:16—KJV). "The prayer of a person living right with God is something powerful to be reckoned with," he said (James 5:16—The Message).

How do we pray like Abraham? The life we have been called to live is not one of passivity. Abraham understood that the judgment of God pales in comparison with the mercy of God. Over and over again, the Bible reminds us that it is "His Mercy that endures forever" (Psalm 188:2). Here's what's required for praying the kind of prayer that Abraham prayed:

+ *Position your life in a "covenant relationship" with God. The culture and business of the Old Testament was based on covenants. A covenant was not a mere promise. A covenant was a binding commitment entered into by parties who had the power to accomplish what was promised. Too often we approach God with no faith regarding His promises and His ability and desire to accomplish what He has spoken.*

+ *Appeal to the character of God as Abraham did. God is always good. God is always righteous. God will always act with justice. God is never the author of confusion. If there is confusion in your family life, you can pray with the knowledge that God is not the source.*

+ *Believe that God is concerned about the crisis points in your life. He is waiting for you to approach Him in the context of a covenant relationship. Christianity is often reduced to the image of pitiful beggars beseeching a mean and miserly God. That image is false. Abraham understood who God was and he understood the power and provisions of the covenant relationship.*

Our covenant relationship should never be mistaken for a "name it and claim it" arrangement or one that allows us to make demands of God. He is the potter and we are the clay. He is our Father and we are His children.

> *Don't bargain with God. Be direct. Ask for what you need. This isn't a cat-and-mouse, hide-and-seek game we're in. If your child asks for bread, do you trick him with sawdust? If he asks for fish, do you scare him with a live snake on his plate? As bad as you are, you wouldn't think of such a thing. You're at least decent to your own children. So don't you think the God who conceived you in love would be even better? (Matthew 7:7-11—The Message.)*

Remember, the mission is possible!

A STEP ON THE JOURNEY

Make a list of things that you will begin to intercede with God about until something changes.

A PRAYER OF INTERCESSION:

Father, I recognize that I am not fighting a person or an organization. The battle is spiritual. I recognize that the adversary is at work, and thus I come to you on the basics of our relationship. You are my Father and I am your child. I beseech you to act in accordance with your justice, your righteousness, and your sovereignty. I believe that you have heard me and that you are working according to your plan. In Jesus' name I pray!

You haven't done this before. Ask, using my name, and you will receive, and you will have abundant joy (John 16:24—NLT).

⇥ 14 ⇤

FINALLY FREE

(FINALLY LETTING GO OF THE PAST)

It's been years since that traumatic moment jolted your world as a young child. You ran to your secret hiding place and curled up, weeping in shame and fear. *How could this have happened? What did I do to invite this person to violate me? How will I ever face him again? How am I ever going to explain this to Mom and Dad without them hating me?*

The years have passed and you've moved out of the house—but not out of the secret place. You've kept the secret and the secret has kept you shackled. You have learned to *act* free, but inside you're a prisoner.

From the moment of Adam's sin in the Garden of Eden, there has been a mystery. How can one moment possess the power to mark a human being forever? Although we don't have all the answers (or questions), we all long to live free from the cancer of condemnation. Freedom was wired into the DNA of every human soul. Before freedom became a political ideology, it was a "God idea."

One of the biggest mistakes we can make is to believe it's possible to have an intimate relationship with Jesus Christ when every now and then you still open the creaky old door and descend the warped, squeaky stairs down into the darkness to relive the moment. By doing this, you're stepping out of the blessed space of *now* and re-entering the terrible, painful past. You hate going there, but it calls you back again and again and you keep opening that dreaded door.

Hardly a day goes by that we don't hear a story of someone who's dealing with the pain, trying to free himself from the shackles of past abuse, that monster in the mind. Walking with God is all about intimacy with God, but secrets always poison intimacy. Every person who has ever walked out of a prison of abuse or pain did so with the understanding that honesty is the price we pay again and again when dealing with our past.

Living in total honesty has become an anomaly in our contemporary culture. We've become comfortable with extreme makeovers. These are exciting when it's a house that's being made over, but what happens when we try to "make over" pain or brokenness? That's what so many of us have settled for. They've given up on real freedom and live a lie behind the façade of an extreme makeover.

The problem with masks is that they never truly cover what we so desperately want to keep hidden. Something always seems to happen at the worst possible moment and the things we thought were hidden come gushing out. And even then, instead of dealing with it, we push the pain back into place. We've all heard the code words so much that we no longer bother to insist that people "get real":

+ *"I can't believe I said that."*

+ *"I don't know why I keep getting involved with people who hurt me."*

+ *"I can't seem to stop myself."*

+ *"I knew better, but I couldn't help myself."*

✦ *"Why do I keep pushing away the people who really love me?"*

On what seemed like an ordinary day in the local synagogue, something extraordinary happened. Everyone on hand had been coming for years, and with the passing of time, expectancy had faded. The words being read had been heard before, and so everyone did what was expected. They pretended to listen but they were zoned out. They acted interested, but hope had faded and ritual had replaced religious fervor.

The carpenter slipped in without fanfare, and seemingly as an afterthought, the rabbi extended the scroll to him. He reached for it with rugged hands. He spoke, and in that moment, everything changed:

> *Unrolling the scroll, he found the place where it was written, God's Spirit is on me; he's chosen me to preach the Message of good news to the poor, Sent me to announce pardon to prisoners and recovery of sight to the blind, To set the burdened and battered free, to announce, "This is God's year to act!" He rolled up the scroll, handed it back to the assistant, and sat down. Every eye in the place was on him, intent. Then he started in, "You've just heard Scripture make history. It came true just now in this place" (Luke 4:16-21—The Message).*

The sleepy crowd of worshippers confirmed that when He spoke, everyone was mesmerized by the words. They were even more shocked when they realized that it was the young carpenter boy from the neighborhood. Something had changed—He was older, but it was more than that. He read the words of the ancient prophet Isaiah as if He were the one who was being spoken about. And He was! We call it the Gospel—the Good News.

Let's take a moment to review what Jesus spoke that day.

✦ *He'd been chosen or anointed to bring good news.*

✦ *Prisoners would be pardoned.*

✦ *Blind people would suddenly be able to see again.*

✦ *People who were burdened and battered would be released to walk free.*

✦ *Everything would begin now. This was the Jewish year of Jubilee, when things were restored to the way they were meant to be.*

What are *good* reasons to revisit the past?

✦ *To resolve something that hinders us in the present.*

✦ *To bring God and His amazing grace.*

✦ *To forgive ourselves.*

✦ *To forgive those who hurt us.*

✦ *To walk in wholeness, using the necessary tools you've acquired.*

How do we experience freedom from the pain of the past? First, we must embrace the Good News that Jesus Christ came to bring.

> *For I am not ashamed of this Good News about Christ. It is the power of God at work, saving everyone who believes— the Jew first and also the Gentile (Romans 1:16—NLT).*

> *So faith comes from hearing, that is, hearing the Good News about Christ (Romans 10:17—NLT).*

Many years ago, I read the story of a zealous group of Japanese soldiers who were lost in the thick jungles of the Philippines during World War II. While they were stalking the enemy, the war ended. The Emperor had signed the peace agreement, but these men were cut off from communication and didn't know. They were fighting a war that was over. When they finally emerged from the jungle, they had to be persuaded to lay down their hatred, their fear, and their anxiety. The war had ended, but it hadn't ended in their minds.

What the soldiers learned from this is that *the good news isn't good until you've heard it.* Only when we receive the Good News does the battle stop in our minds. As John said, "When Jesus had tasted it, he said, 'It is finished!' Then he bowed his head and released his spirit" (John 19:30—NLT).

The challenge with painful experiences is that they happen to us not only physically, but also in our hearts. Jesus Christ had you and me in mind when He said that day, "He has sent Me to Heal the brokenhearted" (Luke 4:18—NKJV).

Freedom begins and ends in the mind. The battle for wholeness is largely fought in the mind. We're held captive by the constant parade of self-defeating thoughts that our adversary advertises as truth. Push away the façade of each one and underneath you'll find a lie.

Walking with God in true freedom requires that you make daily decisions about what you will think and how you will think. Philippians says: "And now, dear brothers and sisters, one final thing. Fix your thoughts on what is true, and honorable, and right, and pure, and lovely, and admirable. Think about things that are excellent and worthy of praise" (Philippians 4:8—NLT).

The word *think* (**logizomai**) means "to take an inventory." Our English word *logic* is implied. Envision an accountant poring over numbers. Nothing is left to the ebb and flow of emotions. Decisions are made in the context of truth. The numbers must add up!

Here's another truth: Freedom happens when we accept God's forgiveness of ourselves and of those who caused us pain. Forgiveness is the gift that allows me to receive God's promise that the past is behind me. Forgiveness is the gift I receive that allows me to live the "grace life" today. Forgiveness is the gift I give to those who have hurt me. And forgiveness is the gift that opens the door to the possibilities in my future.

Think about the people in the Bible who were able to walk free in spite of their painful pasts. I'm reminded of Rahab the Jericho harlot. After years of abuse by others, she was able to break free:

> *By an act of faith, Rahab the Jericho harlot, welcomed the spies and escaped the destruction that came on those who refused to trust God (Hebrews 11:31—The Message).*

The most amazing part of Rahab's life is not that she was able to walk away from her "Jericho business" but that she went on to move to Israel with her family and "marry up." How far up? Her name is proudly mentioned in the genealogy of Jesus Christ!

Somewhere in heaven we will meet her. She will have to introduce herself, because there will be no scars, no traces of the past. We know her as "the woman at the well." She will recount her story of dysfunctional relationships with men. She will remind us that everything changed one day when she met the "seventh man," Jesus Christ.

Freedom from the past is allowing God to give you the courage to embrace new relationships with Him and with others. Your future is never anchored in your past!

> *Keep your eyes on Jesus, who both began and finished this race we're in. Study how he did it. Because he never lost sight*

of where he was headed—that exhilarating finish in and with God—he could put up with anything along the way: Cross, shame, whatever. And now he's there, the place of honor right alongside God. When you find yourselves flagging in your faith, go over that story again, item by item, that long litany of hostility he plowed through. That will shoot adrenaline into your souls! (Hebrews 12:2-3—The Message).

We never break out of our "secret safe house" on our own. Every prisoner who has ever walked into the blazing light of God's freedom is a living "trophy of grace"—a masterpiece of mercy. The One who comes holding the keys in nail-scarred hands can liberate everyone who has ever been held captive by guilt, or shame!

So if the Son sets you free, you are free through and through (John 8:36—The Message).

A STEP ON THE JOURNEY:

+ *What are the issues you must honestly face?*

+ *Who are the people you must forgive daily?*

+ *Who are the people you can trust to "hold your trampoline"?*

+ *What are the caution lights you need to observe?*

+ *Who are the people you have invited to pray for you?*

+ *Who are the people who can correct you?*

+ *Who are the people who will celebrate with you?*

∻ 15 ∻

THE MYSTERY OF R.H. DAMON

(THERE IS A STORY WAITING TO BE TOLD)

Because of that obedience, God lifted him high and honored him
far beyond anyone or anything, ever, so that all created beings
in heaven and on earth—even those long ago dead and buried—will
bow in worship before this Jesus Christ, and call out in praise that
he is the Master of all, to the glorious honor of God the Father
(Philippians 2:9-11—The Message).

The years had passed and there it sat, displayed on a shelf at Gary Peterson's home. A former journalist and a collector of World War II artifacts, Gary had bought the old helmet at a yard sale and brought it home, and there it remained until one evening when Gary decided to reexamine his decade-old acquisition.

As he peered into the webbing of the World War II helmet, he noticed the name R. H. Damon. The questions demanded answers: Who was R.H. Damon? What was the story behind this soldier's helmet?

Gary Peterson searched the Web and soon discovered that Roger H. Damon had a son who lived in Vermont. He made the call and nervously began the conversation, *"Please don't hang up.*" He began to explain to Roger's son who he was but was surprised when the son interrupted, "You've found my father's helmet!"

And thus a decades-old mystery was resolved. On June 6, 1944, R. H. Damon was among the bravest and finest of Americans who landed on Utah Beach during the invasion of Normandy. He survived that fateful day and went on to France. Sometime later, Major Damon was scheduled to return home from Berlin and had his duffel bag packed, but shortly before he was to leave, he was killed. All his possessions arrived home except for his helmet, which went missing for 66 years—until Gary Peterson discovered the name in the helmet and placed the call.

When reporters asked him if he intended to mail the helmet to Vermont, Peterson said he intended to deliver it in person so he could personally express the gratitude of a nation for the bravery of R.H. Damon and others like him, men and women who walked away from the comforts of America and paid the ultimate price on distant battlefields.[7]

The words of the late President Ronald Reagan, delivered on the 40th anniversary of D-day in Normandy, France, sum up our collective gratitude:

> *And behind me is a memorial that symbolizes the Ranger daggers that were thrust into the top of these cliffs. And before me are the men who put them there. These are the boys of Pointe du Hoc. These are the men who took the cliffs. These are the champions who helped free a continent. And these are the heroes who helped end a war. Gentlemen, I look at you and I think of the words of Stephen Spender's poem. You are men who in your "lives fought for life and left the vivid air signed with your honor."*

As I have reflected on the story of R.H. Damon, I have discovered a few insights about walking with God. First, if you have made the commitment to walk with God, you must embrace the fact that sometimes it seems that He is never in a hurry.

Why did it require 40 years in the wilderness? It's a known fact that the journey from Egypt to Israel was relatively short, so why the long wilderness journey? Walking with God can never be hurried. God is the master of timing. We cannot simply trust His actions; what He does is sometimes never quite understood or appreciated in the moment. Thus we must look deeper. We must focus longer until we discover who He is. During my years as a pastor, I have seen Christian men and women lose heart because they were unable to make sense of something God was doing. They became victims of circumstance because they did not know God; they were simply acquainted with His actions.

How do you respond when you realize that the precious baby you carried in your womb was born with a birth defect? How does a perfect God allow a child to be born with imperfections? Until you are committed to a lifelong relationship of walking with God, it will make absolutely no sense. You must be committed to the long journey.

I am reminded of my friend Karen Harding, whose mother was killed in an instant by a drunk driver as she accompanied her daughter to the airport. Before leaving the house that morning, her mother volunteered to sit in the back of the car so Karen could be comfortable before the long flight. Her mother died because she chose to sit where her daughter would otherwise have sat.

For Karen and countless others, the questions will remain unanswered in this life, but they are sustained by the knowledge of who God is. It is over time that we discover not just what

God does but who He is. He is always good, He is always just and He is always kind. This knowledge comes from our relentless quest to come back to Him again and again not because of what He gives us but because we desire intimacy. In the words of Jeremiah, "And you will seek Me and find Me, when you search for Me with all your heart" (Jeremiah 29:13—NKJV).

Another insight I've discovered through reflecting on the story of R.H. Damon's helmet is that we don't seem to appreciate anything that comes easily. Things take on a special meaning when we understand the sacrifices that are connected to the story. Take the struggle out of our stories and what remains is shallow and meaningless.

God uses struggle, sacrifice, and pain to paint on the canvases of our lives. Without these, our lives lack depth and our faith is frothy at best. And just like with the missing helmet, sometimes the years pass before the full scope of a life is revealed and appreciated.

We don't walk with God for the instant acclaim of the crowd any more than a soldier goes into battle expecting to be patted on the back. It's no accident that the soldier is one of the most powerful metaphors for the Christian life. Consider these examples from 2 Timothy:

✦ *You therefore must endure hardship as a good soldier of Jesus Christ (2 Timothy 2:3—NKJV).*

✦ *No one engaged in warfare entangles himself with the affairs of this life, that he may please him who enlisted him as a soldier (2 Timothy 2:4—NKJV).*

Soldiers answer the call of duty. Soldiers leave home. They say goodbye to family and boldly engage the enemy with no thought of parades, cheers, or glory. For you, the call of duty may mean leaving a comfortable job with benefits. For someone else, it might be the challenge of letting go of old friendships. Often, we are compelled to leave the known for the unknown. This is the steep price we sometimes pay to enter a deeper spiritual life.

The nameless helmet was just that—a helmet—but the moment the name is connected with a face and a story, we're filled with a greater appreciation for the enormous price paid by one soldier and *all* soldiers who lost their lives.

We can never truly walk with God without a deep appreciation for the enormous sacrifice that God made on our behalf. The thing that causes the Christian's faith to come alive is knowing the Christ who hung on the cross when we were far from God.

Think of yourselves the way Christ Jesus thought of himself. He had equal status with God but didn't think so much of himself that he had to cling to the advantages of that status no matter what. Not at all. When the time came, he set aside the privileges of deity and took on the status of a slave, became human! Having become human, he stayed human. It was an incredibly humbling process. He didn't claim special privileges. Instead, he lived a selfless, obedient life and then died a selfless, obedient death—and the worst kind of death at that—a crucifixion (Philippians 2:5-8—The Message).

The children of Israel who walked across the dry ground of the Jordon did so with the understanding that they did not arrive into the land because of their own ability. They arrived in the promised land because God was their "promise-keeper."

How do you keep the story alive from generation to generation? God instituted the Passover to keep the story alive.

The people who lived close to the Jews could never quite understand and appreciate the yearly feast of Passover. But to the old Jewish father, it was an opportunity to tell his children and his grandchildren the story of the long journey.

The remarkable story included the pain of Egypt, the miraculous march across the Red Sea, and the miracles that occurred along the way. Finally there was the crossing of the Jordan into the Promise Land. Listen carefully during Passover and you'll hear the rabbi: "This is why we celebrate, this is why we are grateful!"

We read the book of Job, and while we appreciate the narrative, we find it hard to buy into a God who allowed Job to lose everything. His wife insisted that he curse God and die. His three friends (or accusers) berated him with the idea that he must have been a fraud. Surely he had done something to cause the anger of God to be unleashed on him. By the time you reach the last chapter, you're exhausted, but then you read:

> *And the LORD restored Job's losses when he prayed for his friends. Indeed the LORD gave Job twice as much as he had before. Then all his brothers, all his sisters, and all those who had been his acquaintances before, came to him and ate food with him in his house; and they consoled him and comforted him for all the adversity that the LORD had brought upon him. Each one gave him a piece of silver and each a ring of gold. Now the LORD blessed the latter days of Job more than the beginning.... After this Job lived one hundred and forty years, and saw his children and grandchildren for four generations. So Job died, old and full of days (Job 42:10-16—NKJV).*

If you were privileged to live in the same neighborhood as Job, you would have noticed that the elderly gentleman walking down the path with his grandchildren had a special aura about him. This wasn't just an old man who was proud of his rambunctious grandkids. This was Job. Not the Job of chapter one but the Job of chapter 46. To appreciate the Job of chapter 46, you have to read his story, and the next time you do, remember that Job lived through all of it!

My last insight is that walking with God is meaningless unless we allow God to force us to pause every now and then to appreciate the fact that the privileges we sometimes take for granted were purchased at a high price. Without a heart of gratitude, we can never really have a heart of worship.

Thousands of helmets were issued during World War II, but this one was special because a name was attached to it. We hear R.H. Damon's name and suddenly we're transported to Normandy. Through the thick gun smoke, we see a young soldier running up the beach, one among thousands. Many of them would die that day, and their names would become brief footnotes on an awful, bloodstained page of human history. But it seems that God wants us to appreciate all of them years after the guns were silenced, and so He allows a helmet to remain on a shelf for over a decade. Finally, He reveals the soldier's name—R.H. Damon—and suddenly the story comes alive and gratitude wells up in our hearts.

There is no greater love than to lay down one's life for one's friends (John 15:13—NLT).

A STEP ON THE JOURNEY:

A PRAYER:

Father, help me to walk with You even during the days when I do not understand Your timing. I confess that so often I have sought to see your hand and have neglected to seek your face. Teach me what it means to truly appreciate the price that you paid so that I could be free. I commit to never forgetting that it is only by your marvelous Grace that I am here. Amen.

+ *Ask God to give you the courage to embrace a difficult spiritual assignment.*

+ *Resist the temptation to become angry at God and others when your name is not called.*

+ *Embrace God's timing for every aspect of your life.*

God is too good to be unkind. He is too wise to be confused. If I cannot trace His hand, I can always trust His heart.
—*C. H. Spurgeon*

16

1947 AND THE BOYS FROM BROOKLYN

(This Moment Is Bigger Than You Believe)

We cannot tell the precise moment when friendship is formed. As in filling a vessel drop by drop, there is at last a drop which makes it run over; so in a series of kindnesses there is at least one which makes the heart run over.
—James Boswell

For Christ himself has brought peace to us. He united Jews and Gentiles into one people when, in his own body on the cross, he broke down the wall of hostility that separated us.... Together as one body, Christ reconciled both groups to God by means of his death on the cross, and our hostility toward each other was put to death (Ephesians 2:14-16—NLT).

It was one of those days permanently lodged in his memory. He was a boy of about 13 or 14 and his brother was 16. Two white boys in 1930s Louisville, Kentucky. It happened one evening just as the sun was setting. His older brother called out to six black boys, "Get off this street." A chase ensued, with the six black boys in hot pursuit of the two white boys all the way to their home.

Years later Pee Wee still remembered how he and his older brother narrowly escaped the angry black boys. Pee Wee never quite understood why his brother spoke up that day, but little did he know that he had a date with his own decision to speak up. It would be at a crossroads in the history of American sports.

The player's name was Robinson, Jackie Robinson. It was 1947 in Brooklyn. The color barrier in baseball's major leagues had stood like the Berlin Wall. Jackie needed a willing ally. It seemed he was all alone—until Pee Wee made his decision.

The first shoe dropped at the beginning of spring training in 1947. Robinson had been called up to the Dodgers from Montreal, Brooklyn's top minor league team, on which Robinson had starred during the 1946 season. That spring, the tension was slowly boiling in Brooklyn. A petition was drawn up by a group of mostly Southern Dodgers players that stated they would not take the field with a black man. Reese was the team captain. He made it clear that he would not sign the petition.

The other shoe dropped during a game in Cincinnati. Again the air was charged with tension as men booed and shouted racial slurs at Robinson. Suddenly and without warning, Pee Wee walked over to Robinson and placed his hand on his shoulder!

"Pee Wee kind of sensed the sort of hopeless, dead feeling in me and came over and stood beside me for a while," Robinson recalled in his biography by Arnold Rampersad (Alfred A. Knopf). "He didn't say a word but he looked over at the chaps who were yelling at me and just stared. He was standing by me, I could tell you that." The hecklers ceased their attack. "I will never forget it," Robinson said.[8]

Walking with God is about refusing to flow with the tide. There are moments in our lives when God positions us to do the hard thing. For those whose perception of Christianity and faith is aligned with easy believism, this is a difficult pill to swallow. As we walk with God, there are times when God calls us to action on his behalf. Why? Because we are God's agents of change in a world where the status quo goes unquestioned.

Let us be clear—the Gospel wasn't meant to be solely about social justice. The sin of Adam plunged the creative order into a state of confusion. It's the Gospel—the Good News of the cross—that changes human hearts, and it's the heart that ultimately dictates human actions. The primary purpose of the Gospel is to bring men and women back to God. It is only then that society's wrongs can be made right.

The Gospel was not meant to be enshrined in ornate church buildings, reserved for a select few. As Matthew says: "You are the salt of the earth, but if the salt loses its flavor, how shall it be seasoned? It is then good for nothing but to be thrown out and trampled underfoot by men. You are the light of the world. A city that is set on a hill cannot be hidden" (Matthew 5:13-14—NKJV).

As we walk with God in our technology-driven culture, it's easy to lose sight of the fact that we have been called not just to believe but also to act boldly. With our access to the Web, history will no doubt recount that we were the most educated and affluent Christians since the dawning of the Christian era and yet the most passive. As the owner of a smart phone, I find myself using the latest app. But unfortunately, there's no app for courage. Sometimes you just have to speak up!

As you drive through your neighborhood, you notice the men and women who are homeless. They stand by the busy intersection with signs reading "Will work for food." Something inside you keeps whispering, "Do something," but you're unsure if you can make a difference. Yes you can!

During your son's baseball game, as you and your wife sit in the stands, you've noticed the growing number of young boys whose fathers don't come to see their sons play because divorce has torn their families apart. You're not sure where to begin. There must be a way you could lend support to the growing number of single parents who are raising their sons alone. Something inside you keep whispering, "Do something," but you're unsure if you can make a difference. Yes you can!

Consider the story of Philemon, who was a dear Christian brother who assisted the Apostle Paul by offering his home as the starting place for the Colossian church. Some time later, one of Philemon's slaves, Onesimus, ran away and fled to the bustling metropolitan city of Rome. Amazingly, while he was there, God allowed him to meet Paul, and Onesimus became a believer in Christ.

Paul encouraged the runaway slave to return home to his master, and before leaving for home, Onesimus stopped by the Roman prison where Paul was a prisoner. The two men embraced, one a Jew and the other a Gentile slave, now standing as brothers. Paul handed a letter to Onesimus, a letter addressed to his friend Philemon. In it, Paul wrote with grace and courage. He stood not on the side of Onesimus or on the side of Philemon. He became the gentle voice and the firm hand that allows the tension to be broken and changes the old paradigm. In the end, Onesimus was received back into Philemon's household not as a slave who had run away but as a brother.

The book of Philemon stands as a testimony that the Gospel empowers us to act contrary to culture. Philemon had a legal right to punish his runaway slave. He would have done exactly that but for the letter he received from Paul. One can only imagine the stir it must have caused the next Sunday when Onesimus the slave and Philemon the slave owner stood worshipping together as brothers. Talk about tension!

> *If then you count me as a partner, receive him as you would me. But if he has wronged you or owes you anything, put that on my account. For perhaps he departed for a while for this purpose, that you might receive him forever, no longer as a slave but more than a slave—a beloved brother, especially to me but how much more to you, both in the flesh and in the Lord (Philemon 1:17-18—NKJV).*

Fast-forward to 1947, fifteen years after the incident with the black boys. Pee Wee Reese had the opportunity to speak up and show his acceptance of a rookie on the team. Pee Wee would go on to become a Hall of Famer, but ultimately he would be remembered for more than just his accomplishments as a ballplayer.

They were two boys from Brooklyn, one black and the other white. The moment begged for a courageous voice—a new cultural trajectory was needed—and Pee Wee stood tall. Together he and Jackie Robinson changed history. Every time the crowd roars at ballparks across America, Pee Wee can still be heard.

> *'Tis the human touch in this world that counts,*
> *The touch of your hand and mine,*
> *Which means far more to the fainting heart*
> *Than shelter and bread and wine;*
> *For shelter is gone when the night is o'er,*
> *And bread lasts only a day,*
> *But the touch of the hand and the sound of the voice*
> *Sing on in the soul always-*
> *—from* The Human Touch, *by Spenser Michael Free*

A STEP ON THE JOURNEY:

Finding the courage to stand isn't always easy. Here are a few lessons from the book of Philemon:

+ *The most powerful words we can speak are our actions.*

+ *It is in the crucible of a tense moment that we come to terms with our courage.*

+ *We ultimately live and act out of our convictions.*

+ *Convictions are never cheap.*

+ *Like Pee Wee, when we act courageously, we challenge the status quo and allow others to see God's perspective.*

+ *We're never certain of the price of standing firm, but we must be prepared to pay the price.*

❧ 17 ❧

HAZARDOUS JOURNEY... SAFELY HOME

(Saying Yes to the Epic Journey)

*Here's to the crazy ones. The rebels. The troublemakers.
The ones who see things differently. While some may see them as
the crazy ones, we see genius. Because the people who are crazy
enough to think they can change the world are the ones who do.*
—Steve Jobs

*It was by faith that Abraham obeyed when God called him to leave
home and go to another land that God would give him as his inheritance.
He went without knowing where he was going....Abraham was
confidently looking forward to a city with eternal foundations,
a city designed and built by God (Hebrews 11:8-10—NLT).*

It was the sort of ad that could have been easily missed during that dreary time in London. Who would waste money putting that kind of advertisement in the paper? Times were tough. Jobs were scarce. Those who were lucky enough to have a job would have been crazy to even give it a second thought.

It read: "Men wanted for Hazardous Journey. Small wages, bitter cold, long months of complete darkness, constant danger, safe return doubtful. Honor and recognition in case of success."

Sir Ernest Shackleton had placed the ad. An experienced explorer, he dreamed of leading a group of men. The plan was to sail to Antarctica and then journey on foot 1,800 miles across uncharted glaciers and mountain ranges.

Believe it or not, thousands of men responded! Twenty-eight would eventually set sail for a "frozen hell."

History records that in December 1914, Shackleton and his crew set out on what would be a terrifying adventure. Ironically, the name of the ship was "Endurance," which Shackleton named after his family motto: *Fortitudine Vincimus* ("by endurance we conquer").

Trouble became their sailing companion early in the voyage. The wooden vessel was trapped in the ice pack of the Weddell Sea for 10 months until the ship broke apart—a harbinger of what was to follow. The crew was able to escape but was left stranded on ice floats for five months of bitter cold. Later, the men were able to use the three small lifeboats to sail to Elephant Island.

Some 497 days later, they were stranded on a deserted island, which because of its distance from the shipping lanes offered little hope that they would be rescued. When Shackleton realized the magnitude of their plight, he and five others set out on what would be a 17-day, 800-mile journey through some of the world's deadliest seas to South Georgia Island, where a whaling station was located.

The six men arrived on an uninhabited part of the island. To reach the station, they had to cross 26 miles of glaciers and mountains that were considered impassable.

We do not walk with God because we are given the "right" set of guarantees. We walk with God because we respond to the deep longing of our hearts to be fully alive, to live a life where each day has its challenges and rewards. It seems that the human heart wasn't meant to behave rationally in every situation.

We walk with God just like the ancients who saw the bigger picture. They saw the "road less traveled" and answered the inner longing of their hearts to trust God's ability to keep them safe. Remove faith from their stories and Abraham would have remained just another idol-worshipper in Ur of the Chaldees. Moses would have taken his place as one of the Pharaohs of ancient Egypt.

Remove the "faith factor" and the courageous band of brothers—Daniel, Shadrach, Meshach and Abednego—would simply have been four brilliant Hebrews who quickly assimilated into the culture of Babylon.

Maybe you've become disheartened in your walk with God. You've suffered a severe financial setback because of the economy. Maybe you're one of the millions who have seen their homes go into foreclosure. You're now left wondering if you bought into the wrong concept of God. It's been painful. You're dealing with the stark reality that walking with God is no cakewalk. Bad things happen to good Christians!

We can walk with God successfully only when we understand that the blessing is Christ. He is the answer. This kingdom we are promised is not an external one but a kingdom within. We learn these difficult lessons only on the hazardous journey with God.

One of the finest men I ever had the privilege of pastoring was Lieutenant Colonel Jimmy Lewis. He was a godly, gentle, unassuming sort of a man, and I had hoped Jimmy would always be in my life. He was our church's head usher, but he was more than that. He was my chief encourager. Jimmy was diagnosed with brain cancer, and I still struggle to understand why God chose to invite Jimmy to join Him on the journey of suffering. I would have done anything to abort Jimmy's adventure into the abyss of brain cancer, but he was a soldier and he faced the unknown of his disease armed with his faith.

In the middle of his journey, I had a front-row seat. I was able to see a courageous soldier fight the battle with cancer and never lose his faith. He served our church for as long as he could. As his fight progressed, he was unable to attend services, but his heart was always there. During our visits together, it was clear that he was fearless. He believed that God was his healer whether he lived or died. He was prepared for either.

During my final visit with Jimmy, I realized he was not dying of cancer; he was dying "in faith." On a peaceful August morning, Jimmy arrived home safely. He is now awaiting all of us who are walking with God.

Walking with God is:

+ *Trusting God to lead us to places at the edge of our ability.*

+ *Being able to deal with the unexpected and unplanned challenges to our faith.*

+ *Realizing that even with our best efforts, there are no guarantees of success.*

+ *Believing that life at its best wasn't meant to be lived in the safety zone.*

+ *Refusing to lose hope when everything seems hopeless.*

+ *Possessing the confidence that we will arrive safely home.*

In case you're wondering how Shackleton's adventure concluded, he was able to return and rescue the remainder of his men from Elephant Island despite the hardships. The most amazing part of the journey was that not one of the 28-member crew was lost. They returned home safely to tell of their hazardous adventure.

For Christians, the end of our journey walking with God will be heaven. It is impossible for the human mind to fully grasp the atmosphere that will permeate the place the Bible calls the New Jerusalem, but Revelation gives us an idea:

> *He'll wipe every tear from their eyes. Death is gone for good—tears gone, crying gone, pain gone—all the first order of things gone (Revelation 21:5—The Message).*

What we know for sure is that heaven will be a gathering of heroes. It will be a coming together of God's children. Each will tell his or her unique story of walking with God. Daniel will tell of his adventure in a lion's den. The giant-slayer, David, will recount his epic battle with the 9-foot-tall Goliath. Jonah will have the biggest "fish story," a tale of stormy seas, the ride of his life in the belly of a whale, and ultimately God's display of grace to people who did not deserve grace.

My wife and I will tell of our journey from Stockton, California, to Reston, Virginia, as crazy church planters. Like the men who followed Shackleton, we followed the Holy Spirit out of our comfort zone. We will tell our story of strength in spite of our weaknesses. We will tell how God enabled us to build His church!

And you—you will tell your story. It will be sprinkled with successes and setbacks, hope and heartbreak, and it will end with how you arrived safely home after an epic adventure, walking with God.

All these people died still believing what God had promised them. They did not receive what was promised, but they saw it all from a distance and welcomed it. They agreed that they were foreigners and nomads here on earth. Obviously people who say such things are looking forward to a country they can call their own. If they had longed for the country they came from, they could have gone back. But they were looking for a better place, a heavenly homeland. That is why God is not ashamed to be called their God, for he has prepared a city for them (Hebrews 11:13-16—NLT).

In Sir Ernest Shackleton's case, conventional wisdom proved to be wrong. There *were* men in London who wanted the kind of adventure he was offering. The drudgery and the daily grind of a secure factory job wasn't enough. There had to be more to life. And thus a little ad brought out the crazy people.

Today, the Holy Spirit is still beckoning the hearts of "crazy people" to leave the comfortable places and set sail for the spiritual unknown. How will you respond? If you say "yes," you will discover a whole new world. A life spent walking with God.

A STEP ON THE JOURNEY:

What has the Holy Spirit prompted you to do?
What are the things holding you back from acting in faith?
What would your life look like if you were doing what God has asked you to do?

I, Jesus, have sent my angel to give you this message.... The Spirit and the bride say, 'Come.' Let anyone who hears this say, 'Come.' Let anyone who is thirsty come (Revelation 22:16-17—NLT).

✦ 18 ✦

DEEPER

(An Invitation Into the Supernatural)

*I don't want a minimal life! I want to understand
the main thing about life & pursue it.*
—*John Piper*, Don't Waste Your Life

*It is the nature of stone to be satisfied. It is the nature
of water to want to be somewhere else.*
—*from the poem* Gravel, *by Mary Oliver*

W e've all heard the stories of successful executives, entrepreneurs, or just ordinary people who decided to walk away from their "envied lives" and live out the longing of their inner selves. We often quickly dismiss their actions as simply the impulsive knee-jerk response of people who will probably come to their senses later. We expect that sooner or later, they will wander back to join the "regular rats" in the race—a.k.a. the "normal life."

Thomas Kelley was a Quaker missionary. He captured our inner longing for a deeper life:

*We feel honestly the pull of many obligations and try to fulfill
them all. And we are unhappy, uneasy, strained, oppressed,
and fearful we shall be shallow.... We have hints that there*

is a way of life vastly richer and deeper than all this hurried existence, a life of unhurried serenity and peace and power. If only we could slip over into that center. We have seen and known some people who have found this deep center of living, where the fretful calls of life are integrated, where NO as well as YES can be said with confidence.

Many of us may need to confess that we, too, wish for a life that has a deeper meaning. Like Solomon in Ecclesiastes, we realize the futility of a life lived for things. We long for depth. We long for meaning. And we long for inner tranquility. A time and place where the noise ceases and we hear the "still, small voice" of the Spirit clearly.

The questions that haunt our minds are:

+ *What does it mean to live deeper?*

+ *How can I can I experience a deeper spiritual life?*

+ *What would my life look like if I lived deeper instead of living on a superficial level?*

"Superficiality is the curse of our age," Richard J. Foster says in *Celebration of Discipline.* "The doctrine of instant satisfaction is a primary spiritual problem. The desperate need today is not for a greater number of intelligent people, or gifted people, but for deep people."

Solomon uses the word *vanity* over and over. "'Vanity of vanities,' says the Preacher, 'vanity of vanities, all is vanity'" (Ecclesiastes 1:2—NKJV). He saw life as having:

+ **No profit** *(vv. 3,4): Nothing we do changes the results.*

+ **No purpose** *(vv. 5-7): We keep repeating the same things and nothing changes.*

+ **No progress** *(vv. 8-11): Nothing we do makes any difference.*

What are the characteristics of the superficial life? We live the superficial life when we attempt to fill the emptiness of the soul with the acquisition of one more thing. For some, it's the addiction to shopping, while the "tool junkie" has amassed more "toys" from Home Depot than he'll ever use.

The superficial life is the tendency to easily dismiss people who don't live up to our expectations. People are cut off after six months or a year. We flippantly sever the cords and discard friends or family members who no longer fill a need in our lives. They're unloaded like yesterday's garbage.

Like Solomon's, our journey through life is headlined by our insatiable quest for more, even when the last acquisition loses its luster faster than the previous one. We're empty. We're weary. We become narcissistic.

> *Practically everything that goes on in the world—wanting your own way, wanting everything for yourself, wanting to appear important—has nothing to do with the Father. It just isolates you from him. The world and all its wanting, wanting, wanting is on the way out—but whoever does what God wants is set for eternity (1 John 2:16-17—The Message).*

To discover the deeper life, we must first go back to the beginning, back to the book of Genesis. Adam and Eve had something special:

+ They walked with God in total innocence. They had no knowledge of sin. They knew only the holy presence of God and days filled with sweet communion as they walked with their Creator.

+ They lived in complete harmony. Nothing in their environment was out of alignment. Everything in the created order was in its place. There was no animosity. The lion would lie down with the lamb. The majestic eagles would fly with the simple sparrows. The rivers knew and respected their boundaries. There were no floods, no devastating tsunamis.

+ They walked with God in absolute obedience to his Word. Each day as they filled their role as stewards, Adam would rehearse the warning of Jehovah to Eve: "You may freely eat the fruit of every tree in the garden—except the tree of the knowledge of good and evil. If you eat its fruit, you are sure to die" (Genesis 2:16-17—NLT).

When Adam and Eve sinned, they lost their relationship with God. Since that time, we've come to life with an innate sense that something was lost. We long to live a deeper life, but how?

As we explore what it means to go deeper, consider Ezekiel's vision in chapter 47:

In my vision, the man brought me back to the entrance of the Temple. There I saw a stream flowing east from beneath the door of the Temple and passing to the right of the altar on its south side. The man brought me outside the wall through the north gateway and led me around to the eastern entrance. There I could see the water flowing out through the south side of the east gateway. Measuring as he went, he took me along the stream for 1,750 feet and then led me across. The water was up to my ankles. He measured off another 1,750 feet and led me across again. This time the water was up to my knees. After another 1,750 feet it was up to my waist. Then he measured another 1,750 feet, and the river was too

*deep to walk across. It was deep enough to swim, but too
deep to walk through (Ezekiel 47:1-5—NLT).*

Here are some characteristics of the deeper life:

+ *God initiates the deeper life.*

+ *The deeper life requires our obedience in following God.*

+ *The deeper life is a process. One level must lead to the next.*

+ *The deeper life is measurable.*

+ *The deeper life changes the landscape of my life.*

It's interesting that we are introduced to the metaphor of
"the river" in Genesis 2:10 and we conclude with the river in
Revelation 22:1-2.

Walking with God is about answering the clarion call of the
Holy Spirit to go deeper. It is life lived below the froth and the
foam of religious activity. It is intentionally moving away from
empty clichés and numbing rituals.

Maybe you're a new Christian. Stop! Before you go any
further, this would be a good time to answer the call to a life of
deep devotion. Envision the kind of Christian you want to be at
the end of your life. What will you need to do today to achieve
that? Resist the temptation to fish in the wrong pond.

If you're in the middle of the journey, you have the miles
behind you to remind you that the journey ahead isn't worth-
while if there's no depth to the relationship with Christ. The
answer isn't to give up on your faith—the answer is to achieve a
deeper faith, faith in Christ alone.

If for you the shadows of evening are quickly approaching,
there is still time to pause. The few weeks, months, or years
ahead could be the most precious. The end could be, and should

be, better than the beginning. There is still time to discover the life you've always wanted. Jesus called it abundant life!

We don't live the deeper life unless we're sick of the life we're living. There must be the red-hot flame of holy discontent. In the following chapter, we'll delve deeper, but before we get there we must be painfully honest. Each of us must answer these questions:

+ *In what areas of your life do you feel shallow?*

+ *In what areas of your life has the Holy Spirit convicted you?*

+ *In what areas of your life do you face increased temptation to sin?*

+ *In what areas of your life do you find yourself living contrary to what you believe?*

A STEP ON THE JOURNEY:

A PRAYER:

Dear Father, I confess that until now I have been contented to live in the shallow waters of spirituality. My life has been more about duty and less about devotion. I have allowed outward expression to become the essence of who I am even when I have lacked deep conviction. Please forgive me. Long ago I traded courage for comfort, knowledge for intimacy, and works for worship. Ultimately, rules became more important than a relationship with you. I now invite the Holy Spirit to lead me on a new journey into a deeper life. Amen!

I wasted an hour one morning beside a mountain stream, I seized a cloud from the sky above and fashioned myself a

dream, In the hush of the early twilight, far from the haunts
of men, I wasted a summer evening, and fashioned my dream
again. Wasted? Perhaps. Folk say so who never have walked
with God, when lanes are purple with lilacs and yellow with
goldenrod. But I have found strength for my labors in that
one short evening hour. I have found joy and contentment;
I have found peace and power. My dreaming has left me a
treasure, a hope that is strong and true. From wasted hours
I have built my life and found my faith anew. —Unknown

~ 19 ~

ANSWERING THE CALL OF THE DEEP

(GOD'S SOLUTION TO THE LONGING OF OUR HEARTS)

Everything about your family spells success. The house, the car, the beautiful daughter, and the handsome son all lend credibility to the idea that you're a family to be respected. And your family's long-standing membership in the local church is just more proof that yours is the family to be envied. There's just one problem.

Beneath the façade you and your husband are exhausted. You're emotionally drained after years of working 40-plus hours a week to maintain the image. Your kids are now grown and you're on the verge of divorce. You stay together because managing the image seems easier than dealing with the reality.

What's the solution for this couple and for all of us who have learned to live with the superficiality curse? The secret is answering the Holy Spirit's call to a deeper life. But how do we get there?

Just maybe you have found with the dilemma of dealing with the façade. You hate your job, but your image and sense of worth have meshed with what you do. Who you are has been lost in a mirage of emotional bareness.

Your friends admire your success, but deep down you feel the bite of "golden handcuffs" that have caused you anxiety.

Because of your bondage, you've been unable to open your heart to God and unreservedly follow the calling of your heart. This could be the moment when you resolve the tension between your job and the true calling of your soul.

In the previous chapter we read about the prophet Ezekiel's journey with the man who led him into the deep waters. In the beginning, the water measured to his ankle. After some distance, it measured to his knee. Later, it was to his waist, and finally the water overwhelmed them. They were in over their heads.

The story is a metaphor for the life we have been called to live. God invites each of us to live with him in a deep relationship, but each of us must accept the Spirit's prompting.

God's promises for a deeper life:

+ *"Oh, the depth of the riches of the wisdom and knowledge of God! How unsearchable his judgments, and his paths beyond tracing out" (Romans 11:33—NIV).*

+ *"I pray that out of his glorious riches he may strengthen you with power through his Spirit in your inner being, so that Christ may dwell in your hearts through faith. And I pray that you, being rooted and established in love, may have power together with all the saints, to grasp how wide and long and high and deep is the love of Christ" (Ephesians 3:16-18—NIV).*

The key to a life of spiritual depth goes beyond church calisthenics. The history of the Christian Church has been:

Revival is where most denominations find their roots. They were born in the flames of a spiritual awakening. Next there was organization. They recognized their need for structure, and thus they formulated rules and procedures. The problem was that after a while, the rules replaced the relationship with Christ. In a short time, their book of rules outgrew the Bible.

After organization, they focused on education. They established institutions of learning. With each generation, they were further removed from their founding passion to know Christ. In the end they became spiritually dead. They preserved their form but lost their function. Stained-glass windows replaced the stains of the cross. Culturally relevant but spiritually anemic. Like Revelation says, not hot and not cold: "I know all the things you do, that you are neither hot nor cold. I wish that you were one or the other! But since you are like lukewarm water, neither hot nor cold, I will spit you out of my mouth!" (Revelation 3:15-16—NLT)

KEYS TO A DEEPER SPIRITUAL LIFE:

Author Eugene Peterson calls discipleship "that long obedience in the same direction." If you're like me, you're exhausted by the manuals and the 10-step programs. When Jesus called His disciples, He didn't call them to an exhaustive study of manuals. He invited them to live with Him, eat with Him, and listen to Him. It was in that living laboratory of life that they ultimately took on His character, His calling and His mission of changing the world. Discipleship is when we become, in Peterson's words, "climbing companions" (Matthew 5:1-2—The Message).

So likewise, whosoever he be of you that forsaketh not all that he hath, he cannot be My disciple (Luke 14:33).

We walk deeper with God through intimacy. The very word suggests that to be intimate with someone, I must first be "into" him or her. Intimacy doesn't happen when people are distant. The implication is that we're close. We spend time together. We have a "heart" relationship. We can be intimate with God only by being into His Word, into His character, into His presence, and allowing Him to invade the secret spaces of our hearts and minds. Intimacy sets its own pace. It can't be hurried. It has its own agenda.

> *Abide in me, and I in you. As the branch cannot bear fruit of itself, except it abide in the vine; no more can ye, except ye abide in me (John 15:4—KJV).*

> *If ye abide in me, and my words abide in you, ye shall ask what ye will, and it shall be done unto you (John 15:7—KJV).*

Suffering is the choice instrument of God for those who are serious about walking with Him. He uses it to test us, to temper us, and to invite us to become like Him. When Christ concluded His suffering, the father exalted Him and gave Him power. God can trust us with power only after we have suffered with Him. (Philippians 2:6-10).

> *I want to know Christ and the power of his resurrection and the fellowship of sharing in his sufferings, becoming like him in his death (Philippians 3:10—NLT).*

We step into the deeper life with God when we allow Him to lead us step by step through the waters of our impossible situations. The journey to a deeper life is initiated by God and sustained each step of the way by trusting His hand to steady us and the Holy Spirit to guide us. The David who stood over the lifeless head of Goliath was far deeper than the shepherd boy singing in the wilderness. Why? God had sustained him in the face of adversity.

> *These see the works of the LORD, and his wonders in the deep (Psalms 107:24—KJV).*

Ultimately, what we really want to know is that we are indeed walking with God. We want a sense that our spiritual lives are better this year than they were last year. We want to know that God is with us, leading us to a place we could not have arrived at on our own. We want to know that our level of faith is deeper than when we began our spiritual walk. We want a sense that if we continue walking with God, we will know Him better, hear His voice more clearly and ultimately arrive at a place that we could not have found without Him.

The answer to all our questions is an ever-deeper relationship with Jesus Christ. My prayer is that you will resist the temptation of the temporary and accept God's invitation to walk away from the shallows into a life of deep spiritual fulfillment.

A STEP ON THE JOURNEY:

I CAN EXPERIENCE THE "DEEP WATER" OF SUPERNATURAL LIVING:

1. *When I release yesterday's failure so I can embrace God's* **PROMISES**

2. *When my obedience is not dictated by my paradigm but by God's* **PLAN**

3. *When I leave my "comfort zone" so I can maximize my* **POTENTIAL**

⤟ 20 ⤞

THE WAY IT WAS MEANT TO BE

(REFUSING TO LIVE A "WITHERED" LIFE)

God made my life complete when I placed all the pieces before him.
When I cleaned up my act, he gave me a fresh start
(2 Samuel 22:21—The Message).

For we know that the whole creation groans and labors with
birth pangs together until now. Not only that, but we also who have
the first fruits of the Spirit, even we ourselves groan within ourselves,
eagerly waiting for the adoption, the redemption of our body
(Romans 8:22-23—NKJV).

I can remember the exact moment when my mom surrendered. She'd given up, and my brothers and I had won a major victory that most young boys can relate to.

For years she had threatened us, bribed us, and pleaded with us to keep our rooms clean. And then the day arrived, the day she informed us that she would simply keep the doors of our room shut. Mom realized that things were just not going to be the way she wanted them to be. Keeping the door shut was the best she could do.

We were fine with the chaos. She, on the other hand, saw the connection between chaos and living a life of messiness and potential disaster.

For most of us, the issues are more serious than messy, smelly rooms. We have a sense of how the nexus between body, soul, and spirit was meant to be. Walking with God is all about bringing order out of disorder. Even when we are unable to articulate the words, deep down we know when something is missing. We were never meant to be fine with chaos.

Think of the messy lives we sometimes live. We move from one mess to another without bothering to clean up the last. Sometimes we walk out of one broken relationship and, without bothering to pick up the pieces, launch into another without thought.

What about messy mind-sets? This is the person who's unhappy in his job and spends most of the time thinking and dreaming about the "ideal" job. The problem lies in the fact that he was never focused on the job at hand. It's especially messy when the last two jobs were supposedly the ideal ones.

We find ourselves carrying chaos. We have unfinished business in our finances or in our relationships. And then we hope God will fix things.

Why would God fix messes when we continue to make them?

In a sense, we sometimes keep the door of our spiritual life shut. The problem is, God is a gentleman. He can work in our lives only when we open the doors in total honesty and unconditional surrender. Miracles happen only when we fearlessly peel back the layers of lies and face the truth. This is never easy.

Some of us have learned to live with the paralyzing effects of fear. We're embarrassed to share our weakness with anyone, and thus we've learned to disguise it behind religious activities, dysfunctional relationships, or the words "That's just the way I am."

For you, the crippling problem may be depression. What began as just the need for a social drink has morphed into the slow destruction of your life. Alcohol has become your partner, allowing you to temporarily hide from yourself. Each time you emerge from your hiding place, you return with a little less of who God destined you to be. You're comforted by the fact that most people are clueless about your plight. You're ashamed to tell your spouse, and so you now drink in secret. Self-hatred about your depression has become an unwanted friend.

There is a way to walk out of these messy rooms of our lives, but it requires that we choose to walk with God. We walk with God through a life devoted to serving Him and Him alone. Jesus reminded us that no one can serve two masters. We weren't meant to be torn apart by the tyranny of the urgent while the important things are sacrificed on our spiritual altars. God is gently calling us back to the way it was meant to be!

Walking with God is about time spent with Him, and yet time alone is never the answer. How often we've heard the lie, "Time heals all things." But time alone heals nothing. In fact, time often causes things to wither. With the passing of time, we may learn how to simply live with an issue we've been unable to resolve. Time allows us to become comfortable and ultimately learn how to exist with a new reality.

In the end it comes down to this equation: TIME + HONESTY + GRACE + OBEDIENCE = RENEWAL. In the end, God cannot fix your relationship unless you're committed to investing your time. God will not help those who are addicted to spending until they become honest about the mess in their finances. If you're caught in the grip of a sinful practice, God's grace comes only when you bow before Him in humility. Finally, God blesses when we're committed to walking in obedience. He cannot bless disobedience!

No matter the challenge you're facing, the Holy Spirit is urging you to act in faith. God is passionate about the way things were meant to be in your life.

As a pastor, I have become accustomed to visiting people in hospitals. And yet, in spite of the hundreds of times I have walked into hospital rooms, I still wonder what it must have been like in the Garden of Eden. There were no flaws. Nothing was out of place. Everything was in alignment. This was God's creative work at its best: perfect, masterful, majestic, and mystical. There was no need for hospitals or doctors, because everything was as it was meant to be. That's because Adam and Eve walked with God.

Thus the spiritual march is a march back to the future. We humans have a beginning, and then we move forward through time and space, and ultimately our journey comes to an end. Not so with God. He is both the beginning and the end. He has no time or spatial limitation. He begins and ends at the same place because of His power and perfection. Where He begins is where He finishes. We see and know God from our limited human vantage point, but in the Spirit, He is the beginning and the end all at the same time.

The movement of everything in the realm of human spirituality is backward, in a sense, back toward the way God intended it to be. This is why we define purpose as "the original intent for the creation of a thing." Everything in the visible realm has a point where it arrives back at the beginning. This is divine order. This is divine positioning. This is divine perspective. And this is divine practice.

In heaven we will be reintroduced to a garden. There will be a river. There will be a tree of life. Everything will be restored to the way it was meant to be. Walking with God is the process whereby we are brought back into spiritual alignment. We are in harmony with our creator. We have peace with God.

In Luke 6:6-11, Jesus entered the temple on what was supposed to be a normal Sabbath day and began to teach. Luke must have noticed the moment when Jesus shifted his gaze away from the critical scowls of the religious leaders and focused on a man sitting in the crowd. Jesus seemed to discern that something needed to be accomplished in the stranger's life.

Luke was not only a historian but also a physician, and thus he must have paid close attention. He immediately saw that the man's right hand was covered, and it turned out that it was withered. We don't know how long it had been paralyzed, but we can assume it had gone bad over a period of time. We also know that the man had learned how to create a "new normal." He was in the synagogue on the Sabbath day, with seemingly no expectation that anything was going to change.

As the entire audience watched, Jesus looked deep into the eyes of the man and commanded, "Stretch out your hand." The man stretched out his right hand and it was restored to the way it was meant to be!

What are the things in your life that the Holy Spirit longs to restore? Open the door to God.

Opening the door means:

+ **Honesty:** *God can do nothing great unless we are willing to allow the Holy Spirit to uncover the withered places in our lives. The temptation is to act normal. God calls us to honesty.*

+ **Faith:** *True faith has nothing to do with our feelings. The man's hand had gradually lost its ability to feel. His response to Jesus was initiated by his Faith in God's Word!*

✦ **Wholeness:** *Resist the temptation to appear normal when things are not in alignment with God's will. Honor God's blueprint for our lives.*

For I know the plans I have for you, declares the LORD, plans to prosper you and not to harm you, to give you hope and a future (Jeremiah 29:11—NIV).

For we are God's masterpiece. He has created us anew in Christ Jesus, so we can do the good things he planned for us long ago (Ephesians 2:10—NLT).

Therefore if anyone is in Christ, he is a new creature; the old things passed away; behold, new things have come (2 Corinthians 5:17—NASB).

A STEP ON THE JOURNEY:

WHAT IS IT THAT YOU NEED TO STRETCH OUT?

A PRAYER:

Father, I recognize that I have allowed my relationship with You to become more about image and less about reality. I confess that healthy things in my life have withered over time and can be restored only by Your power. I now invite You to renew me so that I can experience wholeness.

For the son of man is come to seek and to save that which was lost" (Luke 19:10—KJV).

21

A PLACE FOR BAD GIRLS

(The Stories Only God Could Write)

Grace plus anything is anything but grace.—Andy Stanley

It is easier to save us from our sins than from our righteousness. —Charles Spurgeon

Judah was the father of Perez and Zerah (whose mother was Tamar).... Salmon was the father of Boaz (whose mother was Rahab). Boaz was the father of Obed (whose mother was Ruth). Obed was the father of Jesse. Jesse was the father of King David. David was the father of Solomon (whose mother was Bathsheba, the widow of Uriah) (Matthew 1:3-6—NLT).

The Bible is the story of bad boys and girls. In an earlier chapter we spoke about Lot. In spite of his arrogance, God spared his family before He destroyed Sodom and Gomorrah. And then there was David, the other half of the scandal with Bathsheba.

It's a good thing God keeps great records. Were it not so, we would tend to sterilize the stories of the Bible to fit with our limited capacity for compassion and grace. Sanitize the Scriptures. Remove the "bad people." Rip out the pages about the renegades, the rebels, and the rascals. Instead of a woman by a well, there would be the story of the dignified lady whom Jesus met at the country club in the wealthy suburb of Jerusalem. You remember her, the one who had the great marriage. There would be a story about a farmer who had only 99 sheep. There would be a story about a woman who carefully guarded her coin collection and insisted that she had never lost a coin.

And then there was the father who had the perfect son. You know him—he was the boy who never left the farm, the all-American kid who stayed on the straight and narrow. He eventually married his high school sweetheart and took over the family business. He made his daddy proud. Every Sunday he took his place with the elite group of deacons at the oldest and most prestigious church in "Happy Valley."

Whether we're comfortable with the stories or not, God chooses to tell them with the hurts, habits, and hang-ups of real people just like you and me. For some strange reason God seems to take great pleasure in letting it all hang out—the good, the bad, and the ugly. Consider the words of 1 Corinthians:

> *Remember, dear brothers and sisters, that few of you were wise in the world's eyes or powerful or wealthy when God called you. Instead, God chose things the world considers foolish in order to shame those who think they are wise. And he chose the things that are powerless to shame those who are power-ful. God chose things despised by the world; things counted as nothing at all, and used them to bring to nothing what the world considers important. As a result, no one can ever boast in the presence of God (1 Corinthians 1:26-29—NLT).*

Recently I had a brief chat with a young lady who stopped by my office with her three beautiful children. During our conversation, I noticed how much her countenance had changed from the time I'd first met her. The dysfunctional relationships with men were over. The bitterness, the anger, and the confusion had faded. The harshness was completely gone. Where there had been fear, her face now radiated confidence and peace. We spoke about the wonderful man she'd married and the beautiful children in the stroller in front of her. She was a miracle. I was looking at a work of grace.

It was unusual that Matthew mentioned women in the genealogy of Jesus Christ. Under Jewish law, a woman had no legal rights, because she was a "thing," not a person. It was not uncommon for Jewish males to be heard praying and thanking God that He hadn't made them Gentiles, slaves, or women. Yet we find in Jesus' own genealogy that God's grace made room for four "bad girls." First there was Tamar, who committed adultery with her father-in-law, Judah. Second, there was Rahab, a Gentile harlot from Jericho. Third, there was Ruth, the pagan outsider from Moab. The fourth was the infamous Bathsheba, wife of Uriah the Hittite, whom David murdered after the affair was exposed.

Each of them starred in a major scandal. They weren't the kind of girls you'd want to write into a messianic masterpiece, but God did just that. Why? Grace!

Although we sing about grace and much has been written about the subject, we still struggle to comprehend that grace is a God quality that goes beyond human comprehension. Grace is messy. Grace is embarrassing. Grace leaves questions that can't be answered by any theological textbook.

Rahab's story was set against the backdrop of Israel's conquest of the Promise Land. In preparation for the assault against the fortified city of Jericho, Joshua sent a group of spies on a reconnaissance mission. When it was discovered that the Jewish spies had slipped inside the city, the alarm was sounded. The spies sought shelter in Rahab's house, and she hid them when the king sent soldiers to inquire about them. As the men prepared to leave, Rahab pleaded with them to spare her family. They agreed and instructed her to place a scarlet cord outside her window.

When the day of the invasion arrived, the walls of Jericho fell. The screams of women and children could be heard, and it seemed as if the entire city was shaking. Rahab gathered her family into her house and waited. Her only hope was the parting instruction of the spies: "Place a scarlet cord in the window."

No one in the huddle expected anything but death. No one believed they deserved anything special. After all, Rahab was the town prostitute. Any minute now the "righteous" people would break down the door. The volcanic judgment and the hot lava— the wrath of the Hebrew God—would come down on them. This would be a fitting end to the wasted life of a sinful woman and her dysfunctional family.

But Grace intervened and Rahab's story was rewritten. So it was then and so it continues to be for all of us who walk with God. And like Rahab, we never quite understand why God chose us out of the billions of people on the Earth.

Maybe you've recently given up. Some distant memory has finally arrested your heart. As hard as you tried, you never felt as if you belonged. Your greatest fear has been that if people knew who you were during the wild teenage years, they wouldn't want you around. In fact, you've never been sure that God loved you. You've allowed your Christianity to be replaced by the exhausting effort to do more, work harder, become more perfect, and live by the rules. The problem is, you dread the coverup. You long to be real, to be fully exposed! If this sounds even remotely like you, God intentionally mentioned the names of four bad girls in Matthew's Gospel just so you could understand grace.

After what seemed like an eternity, the Jewish commandos arrived at Rahab's home, and the scene that ensued was downright surreal. The soldiers acted as if Rahab was a prized possession. Surely they'd mistaken her and her family for one of the influential families of Jericho, she thought. No, this was a story of grace, and Rahab had no clue to the amazing future that awaited her. That day was only the first chapter of a story that would span the ages and resound throughout eternity. Rahab and her family were escorted safely out of the burning city of Jericho, and she became an accepted member of Israeli society.

The question we still ponder is "Why?" Rahab had been the city prostitute. Surely, God could have found someone more "righteous" to save.

Whenever we can explain grace by pointing to something we've done, it is no longer grace. Rahab is a reminder that grace operates not because of who we are but because of God's immeasurable goodness and His far-reaching mercy.

Rahab went on to marry a man named Salmon, and they had a son named Boaz. Boaz never forgot the tenderness his father showed to the one-time harlot from Jericho and he opened his heart to the foreigner from Moab named Ruth. Their son, Obed, married a wonderful girl and Jesse was born. Sometime later, Jesse married and his wife delivered a bouncing baby boy, who would grow into a man after God's own heart: David.

Yes, in the genealogy of Jesus Christ, Rahab's name and those of the other "bad" girls are right there in the middle of the story. Walking with God isn't about perfection. God does His greatest work with broken people and weak vessels. We walk with God not because we have it all together but because God has chosen us. Grace!

All praise to God, the Father of our Lord Jesus Christ, who has blessed us with every spiritual blessing in the heavenly realms because we are united with Christ. Even before he made the world, God loved us and chose us in Christ to be holy and without fault in his eyes. God decided in advance to adopt into his own family by bringing us to himself through Jesus Christ. This is what he wanted to do, and it gave him great pleasure. So we praise God for the glorious grace he has poured out on us who belong to his dear Son. He is so rich in kindness and grace that he purchased our freedom with the blood of his Son and forgave our sins. He has showered his kindness on us, along with all wisdom and understanding (Ephesians 1:3-8—NLT).

God initiates Grace. God never waits until we've worked out our issues. Grace is there before we realize we need it. He never waits until we've done something right or wrong. He comes before the mess is cleaned up. He never waits until we're good. He comes looking for bad girls and boys!

But by the grace of God I am what I am, and His grace toward me was not in vain, but I labored more abundantly than they all, yet not I, but the grace of God which was with me (1 Corinthians 15:10—NKJV).

But now the righteousness of God apart from the law is revealed, being witnessed by the Law and the Prophets, even the righteousness of God through faith in Jesus Christ, to all and on all who believe. For there is no difference; for all have sinned and fall short of the glory of God, being justified freely by His grace through the redemption that is in Christ Jesus (Romans 3:21-24—NKJV).

Grace stands alone. It needs no crutches. Grace isn't about the rules and regulations of an antiquated legal system. Grace signals the beginning of something new.

A STEP ON THE JOURNEY:

Pray the words of this song:

> *Just as I am, without one plea,*
> *But that Thy blood was shed for me,*
> *And that Thou bidst me come to thee,*
> *O Lamb of God, I come, I come.*
> *Just as I am, and waiting not*
> *To rid my soul of one dark blot,*
> *To Thee whose blood can cleanse each spot,*
> *O Lamb of God, I come, I come.*

(**Text:** Charlotte Elliott, 1789-1871
Music: William B. Bradbury, 1816)

— 22 —

GRACE: FOREVER AMAZING

(EXPERIENCE THE GRACE THAT NEVER GIVES UP)

He giveth more grace as our burdens grow greater,
He sendeth more strength as our labors increase;
To added afflictions He addeth His mercy,
To multiplied trials, He multiplies peace.
His love has no limit, His grace has no measure,
His power has no boundaries,
Known unto men,
But out of His infinite riches in Jesus,
He giveth and giveth and giveth again!
—hymn by Annie J. Flint

When the brilliant 20th century philosopher Dr. Karl Barth was asked to summarize the many volumes he'd written, he responded, "Jesus loves me, this I know, for the Bible tells me so"

Maybe you can identify in some way with Bathsheba or one of the other bad girls of the Bible we spoke about in the previous chapter. Or you might be one of God's "bad boys," like David or Lot. Whoever you are, you've answered the Holy Spirit's call to come home to the Father but you wonder if you will ever be rid of the guilt of the past. The question that haunts us is "How do I walk in grace?"

Before we identify the steps, it's important to do as Stephen Covey suggested in his book *7 Habits of Highly Successful People* and "begin with the end in mind."

Whether you are a prodigal who has recently come home or you are the "the other prodigal," the one who stayed at home but was still messed up, God's Word establishes the provisions of the grace relationship He initiated:

From the fullness of his grace we have all received one blessing after another (John 1:16—NIV-UK).

But by the grace of God I am what I am, and His grace toward me was not in vain; but I labored more abundantly than they all, yet not I, but the grace of God which was with me (1 Corinthians 15:10—NKJV).

By entering through faith into what God has always wanted to do for us—set us right with him, make us fit for him—we have it all together with God because of our Master Jesus. And that's not all: We throw open our doors to God and discover at the same moment that he has already thrown open his door to us. We find ourselves standing where we always hope we might stand—out in the wide open spaces of God's grace and glory, standing tall and shouting our praise (Romans 5:1-2—The Message).

Now God has us where he wants us, with all the time in this world and the next to shower grace and kindness upon us in Christ Jesus. Saving is all his idea, and all his work. All we do is trust him enough to let him do it. It's God's gift from start to finish. We don't play the major role. If we did, we'd probably go around bragging that we'd done the whole thing (Ephesians 2:7-10—The Message).

Too often we come to grace with the idea that it begins with what we do. The moment you buy into this myth, you're set up for failure. Another myth is believing that once we accept God's grace, it's left up to us to get it right and arrive at perfection quickly before grace runs out!

The verses above make it crystal clear that grace, "from start to finish," is God's magnificent symphony. He is the director. He has the major role.

What would life be like if we basked in God's grace, allowing Him to be the conductor? How would we think? How would we approach our strengths? How would we respond to our failures?

Begin by recognizing that God is the one who sustains grace in our lives. As Ephesians says:

> God saved you by his grace when you believed. And you can't take credit for this; it is a gift from God. Salvation is not a reward for the good things we have done, so none of us can boast about it. For we are God's masterpiece. He has created us anew in Christ Jesus, we can do the good things he planned for us long ago (Ephesians 2:8-10—NLT).

When you realize that God is the source of your grace, you live free from anxiety. This means that God's mercies begin anew today. Yesterday might have been a bad day—you may have fallen flat on your face—but God's grace is here for you today. Resist the temptation to pull the sheets over your head. Step into the promises. "His mercies are new every morning."

Live each day with the realization that grace keeps us humble and protects us from the plague of pride. First Corinthians shows the way:

> For I am the least of all the apostles. In fact, I'm not even worthy to be called an apostle after the way I persecuted God's church. But whatever I am now, it is all because God

poured out his special favor on me—and not without results. For I have worked harder than any of the other apostles; yet it was not I but God who was working through me by his grace (1 Corinthians 15:9-11—NLT).

The man who at one time was the most feared persecutor of the Church had become its foremost propagator. He would proclaim the good news before kings and commoners. He was responsible for writing two-thirds of the New Testament. When asked to explain how he did it, he could find only one word: *grace.* Grace? Yes, grace. It's the only explanation for the gifts of God. Grace is the inexplicable paradox of a life lived walking with God. It enables you to live with the knowledge that because of mercy, you have God's ability. You never become proud, because the gifts are not *of* you or *for* you. They are the manifestation of God working *through* you. As Ephesians puts it, "Not of works, lest anyone should boast" (Ephesians 2:9—NKJV).

Grace invites us to a daily dependence on God: "Each time he said, 'My grace is all you need. My power works best in weakness.' So now I am glad to boast about my weaknesses, so that the power of Christ can work through me.... For when I am weak, them I am strong" (2 Corinthians 12:9-10—NLT).

Grace set us free from sin and allows us to become "slaves" to Christ. Paul dealt with this tug of war in Romans 6. Before grace, we were addicted to sin, but now that we've been emancipated, we live by our "declaration of dependence." Because of our "grace relationship" with Christ, we have identified with His death, burial, and resurrection. We are no longer slaves to the ruling power of sin, because we have died with Christ, been buried with Him, and been resurrected to walk in a new life.

As Philippians says, Grace becomes our ultimate guarantee:

*May God our Father and the Lord Jesus Christ give you grace
and peace ... and I am certain that God, who began the good
work within you, will continue his work until it is finally finished
on the day when Christ Jesus returns (Philippians 1:2,6—NLT).*

God's grace guarantees that God's work in us will be completed by the power of the Holy Spirit. The Holy Spirit is God's
guarantee that the work of God in our lives will be completed
and we will stand blameless before Him.

THE GUARANTEES OF GRACE:

+ *I am a new person in Christ (2 Corinthians 5:17).*

+ *My past is no longer the determining factor in who I am
  (Romans 8:1-2).*

+ *My salvation is secure (Ephesians 1:7-14).*

+ *I am being transformed by renewing my mind (Romans 12:1-2).*

+ *I am no longer a slave to sin (Romans 6).*

+ *I stand righteous before God (Romans 4:1-3).*

A STEP ON THE JOURNEY:

Only the God of mercy and grace would write not one but
four bad girls into the messianic masterpiece. And as He did
then, He still has a place for bad girls and boys.

A PRAYER:

Father, today I come to you again. You know me inside and
outside and yet You chose me to be Your child. Today, I confess

my weaknesses to You so that I can receive Your strength. Today I embrace the fullness of Your grace.

Because of grace, I now lay down my self-hatred. I lay down the negative thoughts that attempt to overrun the battlefields of my mind. Because of Your grace, I accept who You have declared me to be and I now live not by my own strength but by the power of the Holy Spirit. Today, I choose to walk in obedience, in humility, and power because of Your grace. Amen.

⇒ 23 ⇐

WALKING
WITH A LIMP

(ALLOWING GOD TO CHANGE US)

The sun was rising as Jacob left Peniel, and he was limping.
(Genesis 32:31)

You don't always race to victory. Jacob limped his way
to a new name.—Bishop T.F. Tenney

Change is never easy.

An aged gentleman was interviewed on the occasion of his 100th birthday. "During your long life, you must have seen so many things change?" the reporter said. "Yes" the man responded, "and I was against every one of them!" Anyone who has ever attempted to break a habit or change a behavior knows change can be very difficult.

A few months ago, my brother-in law, Mark Schmidt, suffered a heart attack just as he was leaving his job at Loudoun Hospital, in northern Virginia. The quick actions of his co-workers in the intensive care unit, where he works as a nurse, saved his life. Mark recovered, and now he's making changes in his lifestyle. He has lost weight and changed his eating habits. It hasn't been easy, but it *is* necessary.

Change is sometimes precipitated by a crisis. Frank has been overspending for many years. Month after month the sea of red ink has risen. No one suspected, but one factor was the fact that his gambling had become uncontrollable.

Alarms should have sounded. Maybe they had, but they were ignored because of the "tyranny of the gradual." That's when things are ignored because they worsen so slowly.

The day finally came when Frank heard the knock at the door. The police officer had the eviction notice in his hand. With his wife and children standing behind him, Frank finally had to face the truth about his overspending. He had to change.

Changing would not come easily. And it would not be cheap. Yet that is what the Gospel is all about. The heart of the Christian message—and the goal of the Christian's walk with God—is transformation, or metamorphosis, and that change starts within.

Each time I read Genesis 32, I'm reminded that God longs for the moment when we allow Him to change us from the inside out. Having lived the life of a deceiver, Jacob knew how to scheme to get what he wanted, and he had a way of coming out on top. God loved him, which is why He couldn't leave him walking in the same condition that He first found him in:

> This left Jacob all alone in the camp, and a man came and wrestled with him until the dawn began to break. When the man saw that he would not win the match, he touched Jacob's hip and wrenched it out of its socket. Then the man said, "Let me go, for the dawn is breaking!"
>
> But Jacob said, "I will not let you go unless you bless me."
>
> "What is your name?" the man asked.
>
> He replied, "Jacob."

"Your name will no longer be Jacob," the man told him. "From now on you will be called Israel, because you have fought with God and with men and have won."

"Please tell me your name," Jacob said.

"Why do you want to know my name?" the man replied. Then he blessed Jacob there.

Jacob named the place Peniel (which means "face of God"), for he said, "I have seen God face-to-face, yet my life has been spared." The sun was rising as Jacob left Peniel, and he was limping because of the injury to his hip (Genesis 32:24-31—NLT).

Walking with God is about face-to-face encounters with God, and that always means change. Often, we want intimacy at bargain prices—a God who accepts me but never changes me. We want God but not the God who invites me to become like Him daily. But walking with God is about moments when God desires nothing less than a "changed me." Changing externals without a change in my heart produces pseudo-Christianity.

For God to change Jacob, he needed to be alone. Often, we remain unchanged because we're hidden in the "crowd." God loves crowds, but His masterpieces are most often created in solitude. Today, the Holy Spirit is inviting you to a quiet place, a lonely place. Just you and God.

Please note that it was God who initiated the fight. And it was a tough one. We think God comes in a cloud of serenity, but sometimes His approach brings disturbance, in soul or body. For Jacob, this meant hours of wrestling. In the middle of the struggle, he held on to God with the desperation of a man dangling over Niagara Falls. The entire creation had been watching the fight in the dark, and the sun was now coming up in the east. God tested Jacob's resolve by demanding that Jacob release Him.

"No I will not let you go unless you bless me", he replied.

God dislocated Jacob's hip, and still he refused to loosen his passionate grip.

"What is your name?" God asked him.

In the culture of the Bible, people were given names connected to their past, their character, their calling, or the course of their future. A name wasn't just a name—the person and the name were deeply entwined, even inseparable. That is, of course, unless a radical change occurred in his life.

Jacob means "heel-grabber"—a thief or a deceptive person (see Genesis 25). That's who Jacob had been from the moment he came out of his mother's womb holding on to the heel of his older brother (by seconds), Esau. His life had consisted of one deception after another. But when he answered, "My name is Jacob," he allowed God to change him.

Because Jacob was honest with God, admitting that his core identity was that of a thief and a deceptive man, God gave him a new identity: "From now on you will be called Israel, because you have fought with God and with men and have won." Israel means "prince of God" or "God rules."

Many of us miss the moment of real transformation because we are unable to come face-to-face with our weaknesses. Have you allowed God to bring you to your personal Peniel, the place where you see and acknowledge your core identity, the part of you that is small, self-seeking, and capable of doing very negative things to get what you want?

And the Lord—who is the Spirit—make us more and more like him as we are changed into his glorious image (2 Corinthians 3:18—NLT).

Christ has set us free to live a free life. So take your stand!
Never again let anyone put a harness of slavery on you
(Galatians 5:1—The Message).

You have recently become a Christian, but you still find it difficult to reconcile the fact that while you have been saved, in spite of the fact that you have received the Holy Spirit, you still struggle with suicidal thoughts. You've prayed and fasted. You've memorized Scriptures. But nothing has changed. You're at the point of giving up.

Conflicted—that's the word that best describes you. You have a great heart. You can still recall the time and place when you received your call to ministry. You said "yes," but since that time you've struggled. The other side of you is deceptive. When the deceptive part of you is in control you find yourself living a life of deception.

The Bible is clear in teaching us that we are "free." Freedom isn't something that will be granted at some later date when we finally get it right. We are free right now—in the present. The Bible calls this important work of God in our lives justification. It's a legal term that essentially means "just as if I had never sinned."

Therefore, since we have been made right in God's sight by
faith, we have peace with God because of what Jesus Christ
has done for us (Romans 5:1—NLT).

Our justification is not simply a guarantee of heaven, as
thrilling as that is in the future. It is also the source of tre-
mendous blessings that we enjoy here and now. The second
purpose is to assure us that justification is a lasting thing.[9]
—Warren Wiersbe, The Bible Exposition Commentary

For many Christians, the conflict arises because while the Scriptures declare us to be free, we don't feel free. Sometimes we don't behave in a manner that bespeaks our freedom. As we walk with God, we have several choices:

+ *We can live spiritually conflicted while professing our freedom. This is the picture of someone who attends church, professes Christ as savior and Lord, and yet has never allowed the lordship of Christ to be the controlling force in his or her mind and emotions.*

+ *We can abandon our faith after repeated attempts to "get it right." This is the person who walks away from Christ because, no matter how hard he's tried, it hasn't worked. They leave disillusioned and often plunge to deeper levels of darkness than they had known before coming to Christ.*

+ *We can arrive at a place where we're totally honest about our weakness. This is the place of spiritual death. The Bible calls it repentance.*

When we repent, we not only confess our sins but experience what David spoke about in Psalm 51. Notice the words he uses in his prayer:

+ *Blot out the stains of my sin (verse 1).*

+ *Wash me clean from my guilt (verse 2).*

+ *Purify me from my sin (verse 2).*

+ *I recognize my rebellion (verse 3).*

+ *Against you, and you alone, have I sinned (verse 4).*

+ *I have done what is evil in your sight (verse 4).*

+ *I was born a sinner (verse 5).*

One cannot help but notice the deep brokenness that David experienced. For years, he had lived with a terrible and inconvenient truth. The people knew him as the great King of Israel, but no matter how much they adored him—no matter how much they cheered, no matter how many accolades they heaped on him—he knew the truth. God knew the truth.

The turning point came the day when God, in his loving kindness, sent the prophet to confront the "man after God's own heart." Yes, David was a man after God's heart, and yet he needed a place where he could finally face the man in the mirror!

How about you? Have you found your place of repentance? The man who had been hiding behind the façade of royal robes prayed the second half of his prayer: "But you desire honesty from the womb..."

Here's how he prayed:

+ *Purify me from my sins (verse 7).*

+ *Wash me and I will be whiter than snow (verse 7).*

+ *Give me back my joy again (verse 8).*

+ *Remove the stain of my guilt (verse 9).*

+ *Create in me a clean heart (verse10).*

+ *Do not take your Holy Spirit from me (verse 11).*

+ *Restore to me the joy of your Salvation (verse 12).*

+ *Make me willing to obey (verse 12).*

+ *Forgive me for shedding blood (verse 14).*

+ *Unseal my lips ... that my mouth may praise you (verse 15).*

In the end, Jacob left Peniel with a new name—Israel! From that day forward, he walked with a noticeable limp. It was a reminder of a desperate night when he recognized who he was and allowed God to show him who he was meant to be.

Just maybe there's a Peniel for you—walking with God with a limp!

A STEP ON THE JOURNEY:

Take a moment to list the areas in your life where you desire the Holy Spirit to bring transformation:

Make a list of the characteristics of the new person you desire to become:

~ 24 ~

THE GRAVEL ROAD
TO ROBIN'S BAY

(WALKING THROUGH THE DIFFICULT TIMES
TO A SPECIAL PLACE)

Until the age of 12, I spent summers with my grandparents. My brothers and I thought this was as close to heaven on earth as you could get. For a few months I would escape my routine of school and chores and arrive at a special place. This was paradise!

We lived in the big city of Kingston, Jamaica. My grandparents lived in a small fishing village in the parish of St. Mary called Robin's Bay. The journey there always seemed long. The roads from Kingston to St. Mary were paved until we came to the familiar turnoff. We would pass buses crammed with people who were going to the market or were on their way home. The roads took us through the mountains and past large fields of bananas and coconut trees, and then we would come to the road leading to Robin's Bay. From there we traveled slowly on narrow gravel roads that stretched for what seemed like an eternity. Most of the people who lived in the vicinity did not have cars, so no one saw the need to pave the road. Every few yards there were craters where the rain had washed the gravel away, and as the ocean came into view, we had to drive slowly so we could dodge the potholes without missing the amazing views.

What I remember most fondly about my summers was looking forward to spending the days with my grandfather. Like a velvet-covered brick, he was my hero. In his day, Arnold Braham was the most respected man in town—the district constable. If anyone broke the law, my grandfather would arrest him. He was tough, even on his grandsons. But he was also tender. He made me feel special, especially when he planted a coconut tree for each of his grandsons. Mine was right by the gate leading to the house. When neighbors would visit, I would point out my special tree.

My grandmother was slender and quick, her eyes always bright. When she smiled, they seemed to dance. And her voice was fine. If the pitch got higher, it meant we were in trouble. Everyone called her Miss Winnie, short for Winniefred.

Their house sat on top of a hill overlooking the Caribbean Sea. When the wind was just right, I could hear the roar of the ocean as the waves crashed against the rocks. For a small lad, this was heaven, a place where the days ran into each other and the nights were spent chasing fireflies.

As I reflect on my summer days in Robin's Bay, I'm reminded that walking with God is not always about the difficult places. We walk with God "through the valley of the shadow of death," but on both sides of difficult places, God prepares special times and places of blessing.

Before David encountered "the valley of the shadow of death," he experienced God the shepherd. He spoke of the God who was his provider.

Most of us grow up hearing and memorizing Psalm 23, and Eugene Peterson gives it freshness with his poetic prose:

God, my shepherd!
I don't need a thing.
You have bedded me down in lush meadows,
You find me quiet pools to drink from.
True to your word,
You let me catch my breath and send me in the right direction.
Even when the way goes through Death Valley,
I'm not afraid
When You walk at my side.
Your trusty shepherd's crook makes me feel secure.
You serve me a six-course dinner
Right in front of my enemies
You revive my drooping head;
My cup brims with blessing
Your beauty and love chase after me
Every day of my life
I'm back home in the house of God
For the rest of my life.
—The Message

As I write this devotion, our nation has been caught in the juggernaut of a deep financial depression for several years. During that time, I have had the difficult assignment of preaching to people who are still walking the difficult "gravel road" of economic despair.

Many Americans bought homes at a time when it seemed like a great decision. Realtors painted a picture of unending prosperity: "The house will appreciate in value. It is the best investment that a family could make. You simply cannot lose." But then the recession came and the housing bubble burst.

After months of struggling to make the payments, praying, and sinking deeper and deeper into the economic quicksand, you finally accepted the inevitable. The foreclosure notice came and confirmed that your worst nightmare was true. You had to walk away from your prized possession!

The months that followed almost destroyed your family as you dealt with the death of your "American dream." But then a strange thing happened.

If you're a person who walks with God, you look back and realize that you've arrived at a better place. The tension is gone. Your perspective has changed. You realize that the thing you painfully left behind and the long uncomfortable road of the last few years has allowed your family to arrive at a new place in spirit.

Among the benefits you've noticed:

+ *You have a greater appreciation for your Heavenly Father.*

+ *Your priorities have changed from things to God.*

+ *You worship with greater intensity.*

+ *You are no longer living in a state of anxiety.*

+ *You have a restored reservoir of joy.*

+ *You are living in a place of inner peace.*

+ *God—not things—is your source of self-worth.*

+ *You understand that God loves you.*

When David wrote the 23rd Psalm, it was to remind us that God leads us on a journey to places of blessing, but getting there is never easy. Our childish mistakes and youthful zeal sometimes cause us pain. And yet we must never forget that God is always faithful, always allowing us to arrive at a special place.

David knew God during his tender years of sitting with the sheep and praying with his harp. Little did he know that his future included killing Goliath, the 9-foot giant, and being chased through the rugged hills by his nemesis Saul. To top it off, he would survive Saul and become king only to be devastated by his sexual weakness. But through it all, God allowed David not just to survive but to thrive.

When you understand the panorama of David's life—the highs and lows, the successes and defeats—only then can you appreciate his words in Psalm 23. Only then can you worship the "shepherd" who led David. This is the same God who desires to lead us on an unpredictable journey, a life spent walking with God.

Each of us will experience the dark night of the soul. For you, it might be the sudden passing of someone you love. During the days, weeks, and months ahead, you will have moments when you question God's love. God doesn't allow us to bypass pain, but He does promise to walk with us through those moments when our hearts are broken.

In our pain, the time on the gravel road seems like an eternity, but it may help to take these words from Psalm 30 to heart:

> *For His anger lasts only a moment,*
> *But His favor lasts a lifetime!*
> *Weeping may last through the night,*
> *But joy comes with the morning*
> *(Psalm 30:5—NLT).*

A STEP ON THE JOURNEY:

Take the time to read the 23rd Psalm each day for a week. Based on the passage, what are you currently facing and what is God revealing about Himself?

25

THE LONG, WINDING ROAD

(WHEN IT SEEMS GOD HAS FORGOTTEN)

T hese were old soldiers. They hadn't fallen in battle, but something worse had happened. They'd been forgotten. If you've ever had that moment when you allowed the question "Why am I doing this?" to linger on the stage of your mind, you can probably relate.

Once smooth and supple, the skin on their faces was now permanently wrinkled. They walked slowly, shoulders bent from years of long, arduous travel from village to village. Their once-muscular legs were now tired, and their calloused feet were beautiful only because they had carried the Gospel. Like Isaiah said, "How beautiful on the mountains are the feet of the messenger who brings good news" (Isaiah 52:7—NLT).

They had faithfully served God and their calling on the African continent. After many years of ministry, they had finally decided that their work was completed. Aged, tired, and worn, they packed their sparse belongings, said their final farewells, and boarded a ship for the long voyage home to America.

One of the passengers on board the ship was none other than celebrated American President Teddy Roosevelt, who was also returning to New York. During the long voyage home, they watched as people made a great fuss over the president. Everyone wanted to have a picture taken with Mr. Roosevelt. It seemed everyone was a friend! But no one had a clue that two of heaven's elite "special forces" were among them. They had walked courageously with God on the sun-parched soil of a distant continent and left God's kingdom stronger. This was their last trip home. There would be no going back.

As the ship approached the iconic New York City harbor, the sound of the band could be heard over the ship's blaring horn as throngs of people descended on the pier. As the music played and hats were waved and supporters screamed their adoration, the president was welcomed home in a manner befitting the head of a great nation.

Meanwhile, the welcome for the elderly missionary couple was nonexistent. As they disembarked, they scanned the crowds with weary eyes, hoping to see someone they recognized. A few times, they thought someone was waving at them, but it turned out that the greetings were for others. Though they'd sent word of their return, no one had come to welcome them.

Slowly but surely, the reality of the moment sank into their hearts like the massive heavy anchor of the ship. No one. No one had come to meet them, to welcome them, to express gratitude for two people who had devoted the best years of their lives to missionary work. Over time, the people who knew them had died, some were too aged to make it to the dock and others were simply too busy to welcome home some of heaven's heroes for the last time. At that moment, it seemed to them that not only had their friends forgotten about them but that God had also forsaken them.

After gathering their belongings, they found a hotel room. Sensing his wife's disappointment and not knowing how to deal with his own, the man found a corner and knelt to pray. The tears flowed as he struggled to find the words to express to God that after serving His kingdom for so many years, the least He could have done was to have a few people on hand to welcome them home.

In just a few moments he received his answer and rose to his feet with a smile.

"What did the Lord say that has caused you so much peace?" his wife asked.

He looked tenderly at her. "We are not home yet!"[9]

Walking with God is the journey of a lifetime. Some races are sprints, requiring a short burst of energy, but the Christian life is different. In short races, the runner begins with the knowledge that, win or lose, the race will be over quickly. But for the marathon runner, stamina will be required, the ability to go the distance. Because there will be moments of loneliness, fear, anxiety, pain, and stumbling.

Walking with God is about a number of things. First, it's about making a lifelong commitment to following Christ. Second, it's about dealing with the distractions of life. Third, it's about intimacy, a transformation that happens when we walk with Him, converse with Him and, in the end, become like Him. Fourth, walking with God is about not having answers but nonetheless remaining committed to the calling God has entrusted you with. Finally, it's about finishing (on God's terms) your divine assignment just before you step into eternity.

As I write this piece, the big story coming out of Hollywood is about another celebrity couple who, after spending an estimated $10 million on a lavish wedding, have decided to divorce after only 72 days of marriage! It goes without saying that few of us are shocked anymore—inside or outside the church—when people walk away from sacred vows after a short "trial" period. The narcotic of selfishness, self-preservation, and self-gratification has numbed us.

Walking with God is about going the distance. It's depicted in the deeply lined faces of the elderly couple you see in the park. Their relationship began in the springtime of passion long ago, but then came the scorching and balmy days of summer. Those were the days when their relationship was tested. Those were the difficult days—days of frustration, days of failure, days of wondering if they'd made a mistake when they said, "I do."

The lines in their faces also tell of the fall, when the fresh leaves of spring turned a thousand shades of brown and purple and yellow. Those were the days when the night air turned chilly and the winds came calling loudly. Those were the days when they began to slow down a bit but developed a deeper appreciation for each other. "He has been there for me." "She knows me better than anyone in the world and yet she still gazes at me just as she did the first time we held hands." "As he held my hand when the doctor told me that I had breast cancer, he whispered, 'No matter what happens, we will get through this together.'"

When the winter comes, it reminds them that the end is near. But these are the sweetest of days, days spent with the one you have learned to truly love. We look forward to the eternal part of the journey, to meeting again "over there."

Walking with God is about "selective vision." It's choosing who and what you will focus on. Along the journey, you will pass many a place where you make the same decision you made earlier: "I will not be distracted." Distractions are detours disguised as shortcuts to your destination. Turns out they lead to the wrong destination.

These are the points along the way where you realize that God has not called on you to explain every bad thing that you see or hear or experience. But how do you continue walking with

God when a child you had hoped would embody everything you believed in throws his or her faith away in one seemingly senseless moment? How do you continue walking with God when you hear about another respected politician or priest or pastor who has made a horrible mistake in judgment? How do you continue to walk with God when you finally realize that one shameful night that you'd chained away in the forgotten chamber of your life broke loose long ago and tainted every pure relationship you've tried to embrace?

Maybe this moment finds you temporarily distracted by disappointment in your child, in yourself, or in God. The people of faith in the Bible were not spared the painful chapters of the journey, but they continued walking with God through them.

The Book of Ruth was written for people committed to walking with God and refusing to be distracted. In it, Naomi leaves Bethlehem with her handsome husband, Elemelech, and their sons, Mahlon and Chilion. The last road sign indicated that Moab was ahead and Judah was behind them. Who would have guessed that in a short period of time, their hopes and expectations would give way to the cold, dark waters of grief? Who would have guessed that Ruth's husband and their sons would soon be dead?

What do you do if you're Naomi after the third funeral? Do you walk away from your faith? Do you give in to the numbing demon of depression? Or do you pretend that everything is OK and keep your mask securely glued to your grief? Naomi made the strategic decision to retrace her steps to Bethlehem. She came home "empty"—the only bright spot was that her Moabite daughter-in-law chose to return with her—but little did she know that God was guiding her steps. How could she have known that Ruth would marry the wealthy Boaz, that Ruth would walk into her divine destiny and find a place in the genealogy of the Messiah?

From walking with God, I've learned that He saves the best chapters of the story until after you've walked with Him around the painful cures and navigated steep precipices.

> *Then the women said to Naomi, "Blessed be the LORD, who has not left you this day without a close relative, and may his name be famous in Israel! And may he be to you a restorer of life and a nourisher of your old age; for your daughter-in-law, who loves you, who is better to you than seven sons, has borne him" (Ruth 4:14-15—NKJV).*

It is in the crucible of a lifetime of walking with God through certainty and uncertainty—through good and bad decisions—that God leads us into His Will. Just ask Naomi and Ruth!

If you're walking with God today, you may be dealing with pain. God has not forsaken you—He will never forsake you. If you began with a commitment to walk with Him, He is committed to making sure you finish the journey on your long, winding road.

A STEP ON THE JOURNEY:

A PRAYER:

Dear Heavenly Father, lately I have found myself wondering about my journey with You. I know that I loved You in the spring, but so many unexpected things have happened since the seasons have changed. I ask You to give me the strength to keep walking with You. Even though I do not know what the future holds, it is enough if You will keep holding my hand. Amen.

TAKE TIME TO COMMIT THESE VERSES TO MEMORY:

"What shall we say about such wonderful things as these? If God is for us, who can ever be against us? ...Can anything

ever separate us from Christ's love? Does it mean he no longer loves us if we have trouble or calamity, or are persecuted or hungry, or destitute, or in danger, or threatened with death? ...No, despite all these things, overwhelming victory is ours through Christ, who loved us" (Romans 8:31,35,37—NLT).

And I am convinced that nothing can ever separate us from God's love. Neither death nor life, neither angels nor demons, neither our fears for today, nor our worries about tomorrow—not even the powers of hell can separate us from God's love. No power in the sky above or in the earth below— indeed, nothing in all creation will ever be able to separate us from the love of God that is revealed in Christ Jesus our Lord (Romans 8:38-39—NLT).

LONG, WINDING ROAD

When I made my start for Heaven, I could only find one way,
A road that led me through the mountains and the valleys,
A road not many folks could take, when I started out
on my Journey, I left many, many miles behind me, miles of tears
and pain, Miles of storms and rain, this road's been rough,
But I again would choose the same....

CHORUS

Long, Winding road, keep leading me, up ahead I see a sign,
Pointing straight ahead to victory,
I know I must be traveling right, I remember passing by Calvary,
Yes I do, Yes I do,
Although it's dusty and it's old, for years it's borne
the traveler's load, someday this road will turn to Gold.

*There are times when the rocks hurt my feet, my body burns from
the sweat and heat, my strength completely drains, and my face
Marks the pain, my back is bent from the strain,
You see, I could turn back now, but the road is still there,
and every mountain that I've climbed, I again would have to bear,
So I really can't turn back, some may be using my tracks,
I see one more bend and it may be this road's end.*
—Johnny Cook

~ 26 ~

THE GREATEST EXIT

(COMMITTED TO FINISHING WELL)

After 26 years of marriage and ministry together, my wife and I finally did what we should have done early in our marriage: we sat down with an attorney and had our will drawn up.

Like many couples, we simply got married and jumped first into life. The fact that we started with so little might have contributed to our neglect, but we gradually found ourselves in the middle of the journey, with miles behind us. Something had changed. While we're unsure how far it will be to the end of the journey, we're now forced to think more seriously about that end.

If you haven't planned for your death, I encourage you to do so, not only because it is important but also because it will force you to think about one of the most important aspects of walking with God: how you will exit. It's a question we often defer or avoid altogether, but it's one we eventually have to deal with. Certainly it will deal with us!

By this point in your life, you've traveled many miles down many roads. There have been good times and bad. There have been successes and failures. You always knew that one day it would be your turn just as you've seen others take theirs. The exit sign is rushing toward you like a tornado across the plains— an unstoppable force. Ready or not, it comes. Brace yourself!

We're often tempted to admire the most prominent qualities in the lives of the people we read about without probing deeper to uncover the essential qualities that made them great. While greatness is revealed on the surface, it's rarely conceived there. A deeper look is needed.

George Washington is a case in point. In 1781, he earned a decisive victory over General Cornwallis at Yorktown in the last battle of the American Revolution, and in 1783, the Treaty of Paris recognized the end of the war between America and Britain. Washington emerged as one of the most famous men in not only America but the entire world. Many believed he would become the "American king."

The president of Yale University, Ezra Stiles, said of Washington: "Oh, Washington, how I do love thy name! How I have often adored and blessed thy God for creating and forming thee, the great ornament of humankind!"

The poet Francis Hopkins wrote of him: "He was the best and greatest of men the world ever knew.... Sea cry had he lived in the lap of idolatry, he had been worshipped as a god."

In his book *Realistic Visionary: A Portrait of George Washington,* Peter Henriques wrote:

> *The fame and honor he had sought were now his in a way that must have exceeded even his fondest expectations. Douglas Southall Freeman understood Washington's motivation: "Other men might want ships or mistresses, or race horses and luck at cards: his ambition was that of deserving, winning and retaining the good will of right-minded Americans." With victory achieved and fame assured, Washington was determined to perform what he certainly thought was the last, and many since have declared, the greatest act of his life. He would return his commission to Congress, walk away*

from power, and live out the remaining years of his life as a farmer on his beloved Mount Vernon. The voluntary surrender of unprecedented power struck observers as the last act of a great historical drama. King George III declared that if Washington did that, he would be the greatest man of his age. He did. It was perhaps, as Joseph Ellis put it, "The greatest exit in American history."[10]

This is what we find when we look beyond the superficial aura of Washington. One must conclude that it was because he refrained from idolizing himself and seizing power that he was able to finish well and leave a lasting legacy. Walking with God is about finishing well!

As we walk with God, we can also look back and be inspired by the many examples we find in the Scriptures. Paul the Apostle was another who finished well. Near the end of his life, we find him writing to his beloved protégée Timothy from a prison cell. From the confines of the stench-filled, dimly lighted prison, he's able to see the "exit sign." The flame of a life that had been graciously snatched like a brand from the burning by God was about to be put out.

These were his last words to Timothy and to all who would walk with God and carry on the mission:

As for me, my life has already been poured out as an offering to God. The time of my death is near. I have fought the good fight. I have finished the race, and I have remained faithful. And now the prize awaits me—the crown of righteousness which the Lord, the righteous judge will give me on the day of his return. And the prize is not just for me, but for all who eagerly look forward to his appearing (2 Timothy 4:6-9— NLT).

Finishing well has three components. The first is finishing empty. Paul noted that as he approached the exit ramp, everything that God had deposited in him had been "poured out." The picture is that of an empty bucket turned upside down until the last drop of water drips out. Unfortunately, many people die without emptying out—or fully leveraging—the gifts and callings that God invested in them to establish God's kingdom on Earth.

It has been many years since your divorce and although you've remarried a wonderful man, you still hold on to the pain—and with it the bitterness toward your former husband. God has poured forgiveness into your life and yet you haven't had the grace to pour it into the life of the man who hurt you so many years ago.

The brokenness of your home still haunts you. The fact that your mom and dad are gone matters not. You still despise your father for the years of abuse. You never forgave your mother for her silence. But now, just like Paul, you're approaching the final bend. There is still time to forgive them even though they're gone.

You're experiencing a midlife crisis. You haven't told anyone, but you regularly entertain thoughts of suicide. Sometimes you wonder what it would be like to just walk away from everything—your family, friends, the job, your church.

Sometimes the only thing that sustains us through the tough times is the knowledge that we haven't yet been "poured out" and thus God's grace is sufficient to finish His calling in our lives.

The second component of finishing well is knowing you've "fought the good fight." Paul didn't say he'd won every fight; rather, but he was telling us he'd never lost heart. I grew up watching the great boxer Muhammad Ali fight some of his legendary boxing matches. I can still recall seeing him get knocked down by his opponent, eyes bleeding and half shut, but get back up and win the fight. He never lost heart.

> *That is why we never give up. Though our bodies are dying, our spirits are being renewed every day. For our present troubles are small and won't last very long. Yet they produce for us a glory that vastly outweighs them and will last forever. So we don't look at the troubles we can see now; rather, we fix our gaze on things that cannot be seen. For the things we see now will soon be gone, but the things we cannot see will last forever (2 Corinthians 4:16-18—NLT).*

To finish well, you must first finish! Every day, we look around at people we know who have quit their marriages. Young people drop out of college. Preachers walk away from their churches. Sunday-school teachers abandon their calling. Prayer warriors walk away from their altars. The list goes on and on. Finishing well is finishing what God has asked you to do.

Finally, we finish well by keeping the faith—refusing to simply go through the motions. Keeping the faith is finishing with the same spiritual fire and intensity that you began it with.

The aged evangelist Billy Graham was visiting New York City for one of his final crusades when a reporter asked him a question about his political stand. He responded, "I am a preacher of the Gospel." The aged evangelist was still passionately focused on his calling!

Keeping the faith is never losing your confidence that the one who began the great work in you will complete on the day of Christ's return. As Timothy says: "That is why I am suffering here in prison. But I am not ashamed of it, For I know the one in whom I trust, and I am sure that He is able to guard what

I have entrusted to him until the day of his return. Hold on" (2 Timothy 1:12-13—NLT).

At the end of our journey, those who don't know Christ will wonder how we were able to be courageous in the face of death. If we have placed our faith in Jesus Christ by obeying the Gospel, the final chapter of walking with God becomes our most glorious moment, whether we die or He returns for us.

Walking with God is walking with Him until the day He has finished His work in us. Wherever you are on the journey, I look forward to meeting you at the finish line. I pray that you will experience the greatest exit. Godspeed!

> *Therefore, since we are surrounded by such a huge crowd of witnesses to the life of faith, let us strip off every weight that slows us down, especially the sin that so easily trips us up. And let us run with endurance the race God has set before us. We do this by keeping our eyes on Jesus, the champion who initiates and perfects our faith. Because of the joy awaiting him, he endured the cross, disregarding its shame. Now he is seated in the place of honor beside God's throne (Hebrews 12:1-2—NLT).*

A STEP ON THE JOURNEY:

A PRAYER:

Dear Heavenly Father, I want to thank You for the wonderful privilege of walking with You. Thank you for the twists and turns in what have been an unforgettable journey. Thank You for the many life lessons I have learned while walking with You.

There were times along the journey when I was tempted to quit, but Your Holy Spirit renewed my heart with a fresh sense of purpose. There were times that I misunderstood Your timing, but You patiently led me though my moments of anxiety and fear.

I realize that my journey is coming to a close. I am almost home. As I prepare for the exit ramp, I ask you to help me surrender all that You have invested in me so I can finish my journey with joy. Amen.

↦ 27 ↤

REMEMBER WHO YOU ARE

(GOD'S CURE FOR SPIRITUAL AMNESIA)

While I was growing up, one of my family's favorite things to do on Sunday evenings was to relax by watching old episodes of the popular NBC series *Bonanza*. The series told of the adventures of Ben Cartwright and his three sons, Adam, Hoss, and Little Joe, who lived on the Ponderosa Ranch. In an episode titled "A Stranger Passed This Way," robbers have bushwhacked Hoss. When he awakens, he has amnesia and wanders down the road until an older couple, the Vandervoorts, find him. They are grieving the recent loss of a son, and they take Hoss into their home to care for him. Soon, Mrs. Vandervoort comes to believe that God has returned her son. When Ben comes looking for his son, they say they haven't seen him and begin planning to take him back with them to Holland, Michigan.[11]

Seeing that episode again recently reminded me that walking with God is about the struggle for identity. Every day we're bombarded with message after message about who we are. In our media-driven consumer culture, advertisers line up to tell us who we could be if we only drive this car, buy this product, live in this home, or wear this brand of jeans.

We who live in the 21ˢᵗ century are faced with the challenge of sifting through thousands of conflicting messages. We desperately desire to know who we are, who our "father" is, and where we belong.

We live in a culture that's label-crazy. Labels are tossed around aimlessly. Sometimes we embrace a label without having a significant sense of being. We cling to labels such as *conservative* and *liberal*. For others it's a denomination or a social identification that doesn't actually define anything.

No one took a vote, but you were left to care for your aging parents. The rest of the family thought it was perfect because you were the "caring" one. They stepped back and you took on a role that has left you exhausted and bitter. How do you explain? "I love Mom and Dad, but this is not me!"

For others, the label might be *fixer* or *answer man*. The list is unending, and these surface identities cover over our core identities. We become forgetful, even deceived, about who we really are. When we forget who we are, it becomes easy to be deceived.

In Genesis chapter 3, Adam and Eve had the most perfect life in the most perfect environment. Everything was just as God wanted it to be for them until the beautiful and deceptive serpent arrived:

> *Now the serpent was the shrewdest of all the wild animals the LORD had made. One day he asked the woman, "Did God really say you must not eat of the fruit from any of the trees in the garden?" "Of course we may eat fruit from the trees in the garden," the woman replied. "It's only the fruit from the tree in the middle of the garden that we are not allowed to eat. God said, 'You must not eat it or even touch it; if you do, you will die.'" "You won't die!' the serpent replied to the woman. "God knows that your eyes will be opened as soon*

as you eat it, and you will be like God, knowing both good
and evil" (Genesis 3:1-5—NLT).

Eve was convinced in that moment. She was deceived into
believing a falsehood. Sometimes all that's required for our life
story to be altered is one lie!

The success of your business has brought about a lifestyle
you never imagined. You're the envy of your industry colleagues.
Yours is the story that everyone dreams about. Your success has
earned you multiple homes, expensive cars, and vacations to
places you never dreamed you'd go. You have it all. Right?

Not quite. In spite of the opulent life, you have a hole in
your heart. Every so often, you have a recurring dream that goes
something like this:

You're a small boy. Your family is standing on the dreary
porch as the angry men throw the furniture from the old dilapi-
dated house into the yard. You cling to your mother's leg as she
pleads with the men. They refuse to listen. Your sister is crying
out in fear and you feel helpless. The last thing you recall before
you violently awaken is the thought, "I'm going to make sure
I'm never poor. No one will ever treat me this way again!"

Over the years, you've lived with the trauma of that night.
It's become the motivating factor in your life. You'd hoped
that somewhere along the line, you would "arrive" and would
no longer be a driven man. But wherever that place along the
journey was, you passed it by and never stopped.

Sometimes you wish you could tell your wife and your
close friends that you're still searching for something. You're
still waiting to see yourself as being successful. The years have
passed and you're still looking, still trying to find out who you
are. Success hasn't made you feel successful. Inside you're angry.

The unquenchable yearning for more has made you a chameleon, a changeling.

You're out of control. Life has become a game of exchanging one mask for another. In the process, you've lost the most valuable thing: you.

Walking with God is reclaiming and embracing the truth about who you are and who God meant for you to be. This is the truth that matters. This is the truth that ultimately sets you free.

Luke 15 has been called the greatest chapter of the Bible. In it, Jesus uses three stories to teach one great truth. In the first, a farmer is counting his sheep as they pass under his staff at the end of the day. When the last sheep has passed safely into the fold, he realizes that one is still missing. Frantic, he looks for it, but he can't find it. He decides to leave the 99 other sheep to go searching for the one that's lost. Searching through the night, he finally finds it.

Jesus then tells of a woman who has 10 silver coins. One day she notices that one is missing, and she concludes that it must have fallen to the floor and rolled under a piece of furniture. She lights all the lamps and begins sweeping the house and moving the furniture. Nothing else matters until at last she finds the coin and returns it to its rightful place.

In the final story, Jesus tells how a father gives his son a premature inheritance. The boy leaves home for the far country—the "Lust Vegas" of its time, if you will—and promptly embarks on a spending spree. In no time at all, he's broke and has to work for a Gentile farmer. While there, he eats the food the pigs eat and ultimately "comes to himself"—he realizes who he is:

When he finally came to his senses, he said to himself, "At home even the hired servants have food enough to spare, and here I am dying of hunger! I will go home to my father and say, 'Father, I have sinned against both heaven and you and I am no longer worthy of being called your son. Please take me on as a hired servant.'" So he returned home to his father. And while he was still a long way off, his father saw him coming. Filled with love and compassion, he ran to his son, embraced him and kissed him (Luke 15:17-20—NLT).

The prodigal decided to leave "Lust Vegas." He made the long journey back to the family farm. He saw himself as a servant, but his father met him with a ring, which was a symbol of authority. He also placed his best robe on his son, in effect covering his son's past with a father's forgiveness. He also placed a beautiful pair of shoes on his son's bloody feet. A few hours later, the homecoming celebration began.

Jesus took time in Luke 15 to tell one parable with three different movements, but they all had a common thread. In each, something of value was lost, the thing that was lost mattered to someone, a search was made and its ultimate retrieval brought rejoicing.

Speaking of parables, how does that *Bonanza* episode end? The tension comes to a climax when Ben discovers his son living at the Vandervoorts' house. When confronted about their lie, they argue that Hoss had no memory of his former life and thus must be respected in his choice to return home with his "new" family.

Hoss and the Vandervoorts spend the night before their trip at the Cartwright ranch, and Ben hopes against hope that his son will remember the familiar surroundings of his home.

In the morning, as they're ready to leave, Ben accidentally drops the picture of Hoss's mother and shatters the glass. In that moment, Hoss is shocked back to reality and recognizes his father.

As the Vandervoorts' wagon pulls away for the long journey to Michigan, we're left wondering about all the sons and daughters who have forever forgotten who they are.

Every person who begins the life of walking with God will have an "identity crisis" of sorts. Perhaps you've been a godly Christian woman for many years. Despite the fact that your husband has never become a Christian, you've persevered. Recently, you've become discouraged, and in a moment of weakness, you began an Internet relationship. Now you're caught in the middle of an emotional tug of war. The only thing that has kept you from walking away from your family and your faith is the gentle voice of the Holy Spirit reminding you who you are.

Or maybe you're the prodigal. This moment could be the turning point. You're not who the devil declares you to be. You're not who your mistake says you are. You are God's child. You were created in the image of your Father.

Grace has been waiting for you. Mercy has pardoned you. Love will embrace you. Hope will sustain you.

Welcome home!

A STEP ON THE JOURNEY:

A PRAYER:

Father, thank You for never giving up on me. Even when I had forgotten who I was, You never did. Thank you for your unlimited love that allowed me to come back to You without condemnation. Thank You for Your Grace that holds me even on the bad days when I am tempted to revisit my past. Thank You for the hope that You have placed in my heart. My future is not behind me. My faith is focused on the cross!

⤳ 28 ⤳

THE PARADOX
OF FAITH

(WHEN FAITH REFUSES TO SURRENDER)

Among the many brave men and women who were held as prisoners of war during the Vietnam conflict, Vice Admiral James Stockdale is remembered for his courage under pressure. Stockdale led aerial attacks from the carrier USS Ticonderoga during the 1964 Gulf of Tonkin incident. He was the commander of the Carrier Air Wing 16 aboard the carrier USS Oriskany when he was shot down over enemy territory on September 9, 1965. He would spend eight difficult years as a POW.

After his release, Stockdale was asked how he survived. His response hands us a great truth that applies to our walk with God: "I never lost faith in the end of the story. I never doubted not only that we would get out, but also that I would prevail in the end and turn the experience into the defining event in my life, which, in retrospect, I would not trade."

"Who didn't make it out?" the reporter then asked.

"Oh, that's easy," Stockdale replied. "The optimists. They were the ones who said, 'We're going to be out by Christmas.' And Christmas would come and go. Then they'd say, 'We're going to be out by Easter.' And Easter would come and Easter would go. And then Thanksgiving, and then it would be Christmas again. And they died of a broken heart."[12]

Stockdale's approach to the situation has come to be known as "the Stockdale paradox." It amounts to maintaining the right perspective, holding on to hope for the future while honestly confronting the current reality.

Walking with God is about maintaining the right perspective. Our faith allows us to face the current realities of life and yet never cease trusting that God will provide a better future.

In some circles, the concept of faith has been contaminated and no longer represents the teaching of Scripture. When the word *faith* is mentioned, it's often within the context of the American paradigm, aligned with a story in which someone is headed for disaster and confidently "commands" God to act. Invariably, God arrives in Lone Ranger fashion and saves the day just in time. Invariably, the ending is happy and neat.

What of the other side of faith? Yes, the other side, the side that leaves us wondering why God didn't answer in the way we'd prayed for. The side that leaves us wondering why a loved one died.

The Book of Daniel is a reminder of faith's finest hour. It's faith with combat boots on. It's not faith in faith. It's faith in God. There's a difference.

Faith in faith is the belief that if I pray enough or fast enough or if I'm good enough, bad things won't happen; God will always act in the way I instruct him. Faith in God is confidence in the character of God. It's having the perspective that Stockdale embraced. He believed he had the inner strength to survive, and in the end, he thrived despite his difficulties. His faith also allowed him to trust God's timing. He understood that he might not be home for Christmas.

The names Shadrach, Meshach, and Abednego are reminders of this paradox of faith. In Daniel chapter 3, they face the dilemma that people of faith ultimately must confront. The three Hebrews were among the captives carried off into captivity, and they refused to bow to King Nebuchadnezzar's image. Here's how they responded when asked to reconsider:

> *Oh Nebuchadnezzar, we have no need to answer you in this matter. If that is the case, our God whom we serve is able to deliver us from the burning fiery furnace and He will deliver us from your hand, O king. But if not, let it be known to you, O king, that we do not serve your gods, nor will we worship the golden image which you have set up (Daniel 3:16-18—NKJV).*

Here's the perspective of faith:

1. *We are not pressured to have "the answer."*

As a young pastor, I would dread the times when I had to visit a member of our congregation who was dying. The tension I felt might be summed up by the question "How do we reconcile our faith in God as a healer when, in spite of our prayers, people die?"

It was later that I began to realize that the people who have faith in the Bible do not always live. While walking with God is about walking with a faith to live by, it's also about being prepared to die in faith.

> *But others were tortured, refusing to turn from God in order to be set free. They placed their hope in a better life after the resurrection. Some were jeered at, and their backs were cut open with whips. Others were chained in prisons. Some died by stoning, some were sawed in half, and others were killed with the sword. (Hebrews 11:35-37—NLT).*

2. The paradox of faith is "God is able."

This is the place where we place our faith boldly in the Word of God. We confidently confess what God has declared in His Word. Faith is recognizing that God cannot act contrary to His Word. He is bound by what He has spoken!

He was wounded for our transgressions, He was bruised for our iniquities; The Chastisement for our peace was upon Him. And by His stripes we are healed (Isaiah 53:5—NKJV).

For assuredly I say to you, whoever says to this mountain, Be removed and be cast into the sea, and does not doubt in his heart, but believes that those things he says will be done, he will have whatever he says. Therefore I say to you, whatever things you ask when you pray, believe that you receive them, and you will have them (Mark 11:23-24—NKJV).

3. The third part of this paradox is the confession that "God will deliver."

For the believer, deliverance comes whether we live or we die. When we see the plan of God clearly from the standpoint of eternity, we understand that our faith is not lessened by what happens in the present visible realm. Faith allows us to see God's eternal plans.

According to my earnest expectation and hope that in nothing I shall be ashamed, but with all boldness, as always, so now also Christ will be magnified in my body whether by life or by death (Philippians 1:20—NKJV).

4. *The final and most powerful part of the paradox is our ability to say, "But if not."*

The most powerful ingredient of biblical faith is embracing God's ultimate sovereignty. Sovereignty supersedes what we see, what we understand and what we can explain. Trusting God's sovereignty is not only trusting God's power but also trusting his divine plan and purpose.

> *And we know that all things work together for good to those who love God, to those who are the called according to his purpose (Romans 8:28—NKJV).*

Admiral Stockdale not only survived but thrived. He emerged from his ordeal stronger because he "never lost faith in the end of the story." Walking with God is about your story, not just the beginning or the middle but the end as well.

> *And God shall wipe away every tear from their eyes; there shall be no more death, nor sorrow, nor crying. There shall be no more pain, for the former things have passed away (Revelation 21:4—NKJV).*

> *And he showed me a pure river of water of life, clear as crystal, proceeding from the throne of God and of the Lamb. In the middle of its street, and on either side of the river was the tree of life, which bore twelve fruit, each tree yielding its fruit every month. The leaves of the tree were for the healing of the nations. And there shall be no more curse, but the throne of God and of the Lamb shall be in it, and His servants shall serve Him (Revelation 22:1-3—NKJV).*

A STEP ON THE JOURNEY:

Take a moment to make a list of your recent prayer requests. Pray over each one, asking God to share His eternal perspective with you.

29

THE FIDDLER AT L'ENFANT PLAZA

(PAUSING TO HEAR HEAVEN'S MUSIC)

How aware are you of the presence of God in your life? Is He there but you rarely sense Him? Sometimes we complain that God is too hard to find or that He "hides." But that's never the case.

On a winter morning, a small drama unfolded in Washington, D.C., that tells us much about the presence of God—and about ourselves. This is how Gene Weingarten, a staff writer for *The Washington Post*, described the event:

> *He emerged from the metro at the L'Enfant Plaza station and positioned himself against a wall beside a trash basket. By most measures, he was nondescript: a youngish white man in jeans, a long-sleeved T-shirt, and a Washington Nationals baseball cap. From a small case, he removed a violin. Placing the open case at his feet, he shrewdly threw in a few dollars and pocket change as seed money, swiveled it to face pedestrian traffic, and began to play.*

The Washington Post wanted to know what would happen if you put a world-renowned violist on a busy subway platform to play some of the most revered musical masterpieces. Would people notice? Would a significant number stop to listen?[13]

It was 7:51 on Friday, January 12, 2007. The rush hour was in full swing, with people streaming into the Metro station on their way to work. For 43 minutes, former child prodigy Joshua Bell performed six classical pieces on his $3.5 million Stradivarius as 1,097 people walked passed him on their way to work, most of them government workers. Three days earlier, he had performed to a packed house at Boston's stately Symphony Hall. The good seats sold for $100. Two weeks later, he played to a standing-room-only audience at the Music Center at Strathmore, in North Bethesda, Maryland. This is a man whose gift as a musician can command up to $1,000 a minute.

How'd he make out at L'Enfant Plaza? The 1,097 people who passed by that morning threw in a total of $32.17. Only seven people stopped for longer than sixty seconds, and only one of them recognized the fellow in the baseball cap as the world-renowned violinist.

Walking with God is about having a heightened awareness of the "musical movements," the powerful, beautiful presence of God, in our daily lives. The writers of Scripture were aware that we have a tendency to tune out the divine, not because we're listening to bad things but because we're infected with destination virus, the curse that plagues busy people.

In his book *The Power of Habit: Why We Do What We Do in Life and Business, New York Times* reporter Charles Duhigg noted:

> *In the last 15 years, as we've learned how habits work and how they can be changed, scientists have explained that every habit is made up of a cue, a routine, and a reward. The cure is a trigger that tells your brain to go into automatic mode and which habit to use. Then there is the routine—the behavior itself—which can be physical or mental or emotional. Finally there is a reward, which helps your brain figure out if this*

particular habit is worth remembering for the future. Over time, this loop—cue, routine, reward, cue, routine, reward— becomes more automatic as the cue and reward become neurologically intertwined.

Duhigg noted that a significant amount of what we do each day is "mindless."[14] A paper published by a Duke University researcher in 2006 revealed that more than forty percent of the actions people performed each day were not due to a decision-making mechanism but simply due to a habit. Walking with God can become mindless, too.

In his classic book *The Screwtape Letters*, C.S. Lewis gives us an insight into the world of spiritual warfare. The senior demon, Wormwood, is corresponding with the young demon, Screwtape, about how to best neutralize his "victim." He advises Screwtape to make his target comfortable. There is no directive to hurt him or cause him discomfort. To the contrary, the advice is to help him get ahead:

> *Prosperity knits a man to the World. He feels that is finding his place in it, while really it is finding its place in him. His increasing reputation, his widening circle of acquaintances, his sense of importance, the growing pressure of absorbing and agreeable work, build up in him a sense of really being at home on Earth, which is just what we want.* [15]

Walking with God is about listening to the gentle whispers of God.

Let's say you're now a successful executive in your company. Gone is the fretting, the nail-biting hours of attempting to impress the "higher-ups." You've made it to the top. You *are* one of the higher-ups. But the cost of getting there has been enormous. You no longer enjoy your family. Your children have grown up without you. You tried to be there, and even when you were there, you were never quite there. You missed most of the piano recitals. The times that you did make it, you dozed off when the lights were dimmed.

There's still time, but how do you stop so you can hear the music? How can you be sure this moment is worth stopping for? Isaiah 6 reminds us that God longs to break through our mental walls and surprise us with the clarity of His voice:

> It was in the year King Uzziah died that I saw the Lord. He was sitting on a lofty throne, and the train of his robe filled the Temple. Attending him were mighty seraphim, each having six wings. With two wings they covered their faces, with two they covered their feet, and with two they flew. They were calling out to each other, "Holy, holy, holy is the LORD of Heaven's Armies! The whole earth is filled with his glory!" Their voices shook the Temple to its foundations, and the entire building was filled with smoke (Isaiah 6:1-4—NLT).

The passage reminds us that God has a habit of breaking in on our "ruts" with something so spectacular that it takes our breath away. The only problem is that sometimes we miss the music!

What made that day so special? Why not yesterday? Why not tomorrow? Why did God wait until Uzziah died? Maybe God wanted to be sure that the prophet wouldn't be distracted by the mundane and fail to see and hear the music of heaven. Maybe God wanted to give Isaiah a front-row seat so he could see and hear the heavenly choir.

Walking with God is about a daily commitment to be ready. Ready for what? That's just the point—we never know. And we never quite know when or where God is going to show up. This allows us to walk with Him each day with a heightened sense of anticipation.

In 1 Kings 18, Elijah single-handedly defeats 450 false prophets of the god Baal. One chapter later, he's a man running for his life—the wicked Jezebel has placed a contract on his head: "And when he saw that, he arose and ran for his life, and went to Beersheba which belongs to Judah, and left his servant there. But he himself went a day's journey into the wilderness, and came and sat down under a broom tree. And he prayed that he might die, and said, it is enough!"

As it turns out, God agrees:

And behold the Lord passed by, and a great and strong wind tore into the mountains and broke the rock in pieces before the Lord, but the Lord was not in the wind; after the wind an earthquake, but the Lord was not in the earthquake; and after the earthquake a fire, but the Lord was not in the fire; and after the fire a still small voice. So it was, when Elijah heard it, that he wrapped his face in his mantle and went out and stood in the entrance of the cave. Suddenly a voice came to him, and said, what are you doing here, Elijah? (1 Kings 19:11-13—NKJV).

Walking with God is about a journey through the raging winds of adversity. Sometimes we walk through the earth-shaking moments of a family crisis. At other times we walk with God through trials by fire. It was only after the wind, the earthquake and the fire that the prophet heard the still voice of God.

Like Isaiah and Elijah, every person will walk through times of difficulty. The most important thing is to listen carefully for the sound of God's voice. As I write this chapter, I'm reflecting about my own journey. This week marks sixteen years since I arrived in northern Virginia to plant the church I now pastor. I remain eternally grateful that I was able to hear His voice.

How do we hear God's voice above the roar of the daily noise? Here are a few ideas:

1. *Set aside a specific time and place where you just listen.*

2. *Read a portion of Scripture.*

3. *Meditate on what you've read by asking questions. What is God saying to me? What should I be doing? What should I stop doing?*

4. *Write down the impressions you receive.*

Walking with God is about listening for the music!

If you look for me wholeheartedly, you will find me (Jeremiah 29:13—NLT).

A STEP ON THE JOURNEY:

A PRAYER:

Dear Jesus, today I repent for the many times I have missed Your voice because my ears were clogged from listening to Satan's voice. I repent because at other times, I missed Your voice because I was listening to human voices. At other times I missed Your voice because I was focused on my busy lifestyle. Today, I invite You to speak to my heart. I am ready to hear. Ready to obey.

❧ 30 ❧

FROM GENERATION TO GENERATION

(FOCUSING ON THOSE WHO WILL COME BEHIND US)

I am *the God of thy father, the God of Abraham,
the God of Isaac, and the God of Jacob (Exodus 3:6).*

I t was 1904 and Wales was in the throes of a miraculous spiritual awakening. In a nine-month period, something phenomenal happened. So powerful was the revival that the country bars were closed because business had dried up. The police, who were used to dealing with criminals, exchanged their weapons for white gloves. Crime virtually disappeared!

And the revival wasn't limited to Wales. From this new spiritual epicenter, missionaries were sent around the world. One landed in Argentina, where he encountered a young boy named Luis Palau on the street. Luis accepted Christ and, in time, became known as "the Billy Graham of Latin America."

In the early 1970s, Palau traveled to Wales to express his gratitude to the people who helped lead him to faith. Upon his arrival, he was shocked. Less than one-half of one percent of the Welsh attended church. The divorce rate was at a historic high. He found a nation in the crucible of crime. Although bars had been forced out of business during the revival, some of the country's empty churches had now been converted to bars!

Palau's experience in a place that was once the cradle of revival prompted him to produce the film *God Has No Grandchildren*.[16] The message of the film is that each generation has a mandate to pass on the faith to the next. Seventy years after a great spiritual awakening, there were few clues to the glory of the former years.

We were made to be containers through which the life of God flows. We are stewards and not owners—nothing begins and ends with us. We become the containers, or instruments, of God's generational purpose when we live unselfish lives in the context of righteousness, grace, and a faith that begs to be embraced.

What about you? Have you felt as if you don't have a purpose or a calling? You do! Each day, with each person you meet, you do have a purpose. The flow of God through us happens in the seemingly mundane moments. Even when you're unaware, God uses our lives as conduits of grace. Thus each of us can become an agent of generational faith, transfers that are both transactional and transformational. In the end, the sacred march of truth happens more in our daily encounters than in big church services! Walking with God is never complete unless we do all we can to ensure that the baton of truth is successfully passed.

When the history of the 21st century has been written, it will record that American culture was one of the most narcissistic. We have arrived at a point in history where the focus is on individual thought, personal freedom, and the relativity of moral values. In every age, the Church has been confronted with challenges. Our generation is no different, except that we now have more technology, which in turn has given us more access to information.

The experience of Luis Palau reminds us that:

+ *The transference of faith from one generation to another is never automatic. It requires intentionality and constant vigilance.*

+ *Every generation must have its own spiritual awakening.*

+ *We are only one generation away from becoming pagans!*

+ *Walking with God is about transferring a lifelong faith to those who follow us.*

In an article for *Christianity Today*, Mark Oestreicher of Youth Specialties noted:

There are a lot of people who've had this nagging sense that we're missing the mark somehow.... Kids seem happy and willing to attend and engage in ministries, but five years from now, when they're in college or post-college, they just really aren't connecting with real faith, let alone church. Some believe it has reached a dangerous new level. This upswing has prompted Josh McDowell to co-write a book with Dave Bellis, The Last Christian Generation. I sincerely believe unless something is done now to change the spiritual state of our young people, you will become the last Christian generation.

In 2006, a study showed that over eighty percent of teens attended church for a period of at least two months during their teenage years. It said one in four of those churched youth still actively attended church, read the Bible, or prayed. Compare that with the fact that roughly twice as many adults in their forties are spiritually engaged.

The Christian researcher George Barna and his group recently revealed the findings of a five-year study on the lives of young people who drop out of churches. They share the five myths that they discovered in the book *You Lost Me: Why Young Christians Are Leaving Church... and Rethinking Faith,* by David Kinnaman, who directed the study.

Myth #1: Most people lose their faith when they leave high school. "The reality of the dropout problem is not about a huge exodus of young people from the Christian faith," Kinnaman says. "In fact, it is about the various ways that young people become disconnected in their spiritual journey.

Myth #2: Dropping out of church is a natural part of a young adult's maturation. "Today's young adults are dropping out earlier, staying away longer, and if they come back are less likely to see the church as a long-term part of their life," Kinnaman says.

Myth #3: College experiences are the key factor that prompts people to drop out. Here the research confirms that many young people are emotionally disconnected from church **before** **t**heir 16th birthday.

Myth #4: This generation of young Christians is increasingly "biblically illiterate." The researchers found that, by and large, young Christians' Bible knowledge is not significantly different from that of older adults.

Myth #5: Young people will come back to the Church like they always do. Previous research conducted by the Barna Group raises doubt this conclusion.[17]

What are the keys that allow us to pass on a godly heritage to our children and our children's children? The first is allowing our children to see our faith being lived out in practical ways in everyday life. In modern times, we consider teaching to be something that's done in a formal classroom or lecture format. The ancients understood teaching as something that was transferred from teacher to pupil in the ordinary activities of everyday life, such as walking with God. Thus the best teaching opportunities are unplanned discussions at the dinner table or when the family shares a movie.

We can capture such moments and teach. This allows walking with God to be less about dusty doctrine and historical dogma than about a living, relevant faith that offers a biblical worldview that's far better than the current trends. We see this in God's instructions to the Jews:

> These are the commands, decrees, and regulations that the LORD your God commanded me to teach you. You must obey them in the land you are about to enter and occupy, and you and your children and grandchildren must fear the LORD your God as long as you live. If you obey all his decrees and commands, you will enjoy a long life. Listen closely, Israel, and be careful to obey. Then all will go well with you, and you will have many children in the land flowing with milk and honey, just as the LORD, the God of your ancestors, promised you.

> Listen, O Israel! The LORD is our God, the LORD alone. And you must love the LORD your God with all your heart, all your soul, and all your strength. And you must commit yourselves wholeheartedly to these commands that I am giving you today. Repeat them again and again to your children. Talk about them when you are at home and when you are on the road, when you are going to bed and when you are getting up. Tie them to your hands and wear them on your forehead as reminders. (Deuteronomy 6:1-8—NLT).

Take note of the imperatives in the verses. Passing our faith to the next generation is never accidental!

Another key to passing on a godly heritage is setting up "memorial stones." God commanded the Hebrews not simply to experience the miraculous power of God—they were also to set up "spiritual stones" to remind the next generation of what God had done. This happened after the Jews came through the Jordan River and God wanted to be sure that the children who had not yet been born would have a way of reliving the story of their parents' and grandparents' walk with God into the Promised Land.

That this may be a sign among you when your children ask in time to come, saying 'what do these stones mean to you?' Then you shall answer them that the waters of the Jordan were cut off before the ark of the covenant of the LORD; when it crossed over the Jordan, the waters of the Jordan were cut off. And these stones shall be for a memorial to the children of Israel forever (Joshua 4:6-7—NKJV).

This is why the psalmist wrote:

We will not hide them from their children, showing to the generation to come the praises of the LORD, and his strength, and his wonderful works that he hath done. For he established a testimony in Jacob, and appointed a law in Israel, which he commanded our fathers, that they should make them known to their children: that the generation to come might know them, even the children which should be born; who should arise and declare them to their children: That they might set their hope in God, and not forget the works of God, but keep his commandments (Psalm 78:4-7—KJV).

We pass our faith along to the next generation by way of a blessing. Gary Smalley and John Trent outline the five components of the Old Testament Blessing:

1. *Meaningful touch*

2. *Spoken messages*

3. *Attaching high value*

4. *Picturing a special future*

5. *A commitment to seeing the blessing fulfilled*[18]

Recently, one of the women in our church visited Moscow and presented us with a beautifully painted Russian doll when she returned. I examined the artistic detail for some time and accidentally discovered that inside the doll was another doll! In fact there were five dolls, each one smaller than the next.

Walking with God is the challenge of ensuring that with each generation the faith expands. Without such a faith, we will indeed grow smaller until we are no more.

Walking with God did not begin with us. Long before you began your journey, Adam and Eve walked the path. Many have gone before us, and we must mark the path for those who will follow us in lives spent walking with God.

A STEP ON THE JOURNEY:

What are the practical steps we can take to pass our faith along to the next generation?

1. *Set aside specific times to pray and fast for your children.*

2. *Look for natural teaching moments to reinforce your faith.*

3. Model *what it means to walk with* God.

4. *Practice spiritual disciplines together.*

5. *Intentionally introduce your children to great people of faith in your community.*

6. *Be actively involved in their lives.*

7. *Offer them unconditional love.*

~ 31 ~

COMING HOME TO ROBIN'S BAY

(ALLOWING GOD TO CHOOSE THE ROAD)

Time changes most things, but not everything. Thank God that a precious few of the most important things remain constant.

More than three decades had passed since I had traveled down the gravel roads of Robin's Bay. In 1971, I left that part of my boyhood heaven to live with my parents in New York, but it's a place that will always hold a special place in my heart. Home! I've been here a thousand times in my dreams.

It was now May 13, 2004. My mother and four of her sons had returned to bury Miss Winnie. That day, I vividly remembered her bright dancing eyes. She had walked gravel roads in these parts for 95 years, and she'd crossed the finish line happily. I had come down the familiar gravel road to bid her farewell.

As I reflect on my journey back to Robin's Bay, I'm more convinced than ever that we walk with God on the roads He chooses for us. Walking with God is allowing Him to decide how and where and through what set of circumstances we discover who He is.

Every person begins his or her spiritual journey with a passion to know God, but so often we unconsciously want to decide the details of the journey:

We want a successful marriage.

We want a great career.

We want great kids.

We want intimacy with God.

We want the road to paradise, but not a gravel road—we want a smoothly paved life.

The gravel roads of Robin's Bay provided the path for Miss Winnie to find Christ. The roads of Robin's Bay also became her pathway to a life lived in faith—walking with God.

Some of my fondest memories were the Sundays we would walk the rough roads to the church. The building was constructed with bamboo, and there was sawdust on the floor. There were no padded pews, just benches made from plywood. This was where my grandmother found Christ, and this was where my mother gave her heart to Christ. The old preacher, Sutliff Logan, had baptized Mom in the ocean, a stone's throw from the church!

I'm amazed that the first steps of my incredible journey of faith began in such a humble place and along a gravel road! Wow! Never underestimate what God can do in uncomfortable places!

How about you? Is your gravel road leading you into a deeper walk with Christ, or have you allowed your painful path to take you away from Christ—away from the cross and away from your destiny?

It has been many years since you realized that the bundle of hope you brought home from the hospital would never be "normal." The doctors confirmed your worst fears: She would never walk; she would never hear; she would never be able to speak. At first you thought, "Surely, God will deliver." But the years have passed and your faith has wandered, drifted, faltered, ebbed, maybe even slipped away entirely.

God chooses gravel roads—roads that hurt our feet—to bring us to places we would never have known. There are no paved roads to spiritual intimacy. Just gravel roads!

The story is told of two men who were asked to perform before a large audience. One of the men, young and filled with confidence, stepped before the crowd and began quoting the 23rd Psalm from memory. But his performance was mechanical, and the audience was not impressed. People yawned. When he concluded, he walked behind the curtain. No one applauded.

It was now time for the older gentleman to speak, and he chose the same Psalm. As he spoke, people wept silently. When he concluded, "And I shall dwell in the house of the Lord forever. Amen," people rose to their feet. Some clapped and others cheered wildly.

The two men met behind the curtain. "We spoke the same words," the younger man said. "They barely noticed my rendition, while yours moved everyone. What was the difference?"

"You know the psalm, but I know the shepherd," the older man responded.

In the end, the difficult roads lead us to our personal Robin's Bays because God sustains us. At the end of the journey, we don't simply know about God—we *know* God. There is a difference.

I endured the long drive every summer. The last stretch was always the hardest—the gravel road! During the years when I visited my grandparents, I would always wonder why the journey to such a beautiful place was at the end of a gravel road. Every year I would expect that it would have been paved by now. But every year it was just the same. The house still sits at the top of the hill. The view of the ocean is just as it was when I was a boy of 10.

The funeral for Miss Winnie was held on the lawn. On that crisp morning in May, with the gentle whisper of ocean breezes, we sang the old hymns that Miss Winnie loved. Yes, there were tears, but not of sorrow. This was a celebration of a life lived in God's presence. Just as she had walked in faith, she also died in faith.

Her life was lived walking with God on the gravel roads of Robin's Bay. What about your life? What about your road?

No matter who we are, we have so much in common: gravel roads. God uses them to teach us, to test us, and to transform us into His image.

By the way, a funny thing happened on the way to Robin's Bay to bury Miss Winnie. I was by then a grown man of 46, and the long lazy summers had lived on in my mind. But like you, I had known difficult seasons. There had been days of doubts and dreams derailed. There had been successes and failures. Miles behind me and still miles to go, but I was different now. I had become a time-tested traveler looking for the ultimate Robin's Bay—Heaven!

The road was smoother now. In fact, what had once seemed to be a "forever journey" on the gravel was actually just a short distance. The road hadn't changed—I had!

Looking back, I realize that I would have gladly given up the short, smooth road to my boyhood paradise. The gravel road was great because always at the start of summer, we would make the last turn up the hill. My grandfather and Miss Winnie were always standing by the gate!

If I walk in the pathway of duty
If I work till the close of the day,
I will see the great king in his beauty,
When I've gone the last mile of the way.

Refrain:

When I've gone the last mile of the way,
I will rest at the close of the day,
And I know there are joys that await me;
When I've gone, the last mile of the way.
—hymn by Johnson Oatman Jr., 1908

A STEP ON THE JOURNEY:

A PRAYER:

Father, thank You for the moments on gravel roads. Each step was necessary to lead me closer to You. Each mile was ordained to help me know You more intimately. In the days that remain, grant me the grace to keep my focus on the moment when I will have finished my journey and arrived safely home, ... safe in Your presence.

And now, dear brothers and sisters, we want you to know what will happen to the believers who have died so you will not grieve like people who have no hope. For since we believe that Jesus died and was raised to life again, we also believe that when Jesus returns, God will bring back with him the believers who have died.

We tell you this directly from the Lord: We who are still living when the Lord returns will not meet him ahead of those who have died. For the Lord himself will come down from heaven with a commanding shout, with the voice of the archangel, and with the trumpet call of God. First, the Christians who have died will rise from their graves. Then, together with them, we who are still alive and remain on the earth will be caught up in the clouds to meet the Lord in the air. Then we will be with the Lord forever. So encourage each other with these words (1 Thessalonians 4:13-18—NLT).

NOTES

Chapter 3: Is There Anyone out There?

[1] Carl Sagan, *Billions and Billions* (New York: Random House, 1997), 214.

[2] Tali Sharot, "The Optimism Bias," *Time* magazine, May 28, 2011, www.time.com/time/health/article/0,8599,2074067,00.html.

Chapter 6: D.I.Y. Disaster

[3] Craig Groeschel, *The Christian Atheist: Believing in God But Living as If He Doesn't Exist* (Zondervan, Grand Rapids, Mich., 2010).

Chapter 10: Keep On Keeping On

[4] Charles R. Swindoll, *Simple Faith* (Dallas Word, 1991), 186.

[5] Ibid ... 144.

Chapter 11: The Unknown Rebel

[6] "Time 100: The Most Important People of the Century," *Time* magazine, April 1998.

Chapter 15: The Mystery of R.H. Damon

[7] Peter Schuneman, "Spring Valley Man to Return WWII Helmet to Veteran's Son," KTTC.com, November 14, 2011), www.kttc.com/story/15981042/from-minn-to-vermont-son-of-wwii-veteran-to-recieve-fathers-helmet.

Chapter 16: 1947 and the Boys From Brooklyn

[8] Arnold Rampersad, *Jackie Robinson* (Alfred A. Knopf, New York, 1997).

Chapter 23: Walking With a Limp

[9] Warren Wiersbe, *The Bible Exposition Commentary* (2 Corinthians 11:7), Victor Books, Wheaton, Ill., 1996, c1989).

Chapter 26: The Greatest Exit

[10] Peter R. Henriques, *Realistic Visionary: A Portrait of George Washington* (University of Virginia Press, Charlottesville, Va., 2006), 46.

Chapter 27: Remembering Who You Are

[11] *Bonanza*, "A Stranger Passed This Way" (Season 4, Episode 23, March 1963).

Chapter 28: The Paradox of Faith

[12] Jim Collins, *Good to Great* (HarperCollins, 2001), 83-86.

Chapter 29: The Fiddler at L'Enfant Plaza

[13] Gene Weingarten, "Pearls Before Breakfast," *The Washington Post*, April 8, 2007, www.washingtonpost.com/wp-dyn/content/article/2007/04/04/AR2007040401721.html.

[14] Charles Duhigg, *The Power of Habit* (Random House, New York, 2012), 31-57.

[15] C. S. Lewis, *The Screwtape Letters* (HarperCollins, San Francisco)

Chapter 30: From Generation to Generation

[16] Luis Palau, *God Has No Grandchildren* (film)

[17] David Kinnaman, *You Lost Me: Why Young Christians Are Leaving Church... and Rethinking Faith* (Baker, Grand Rapids, Mich., 2011)

[18] Gary Smalley, John Trent, *The Blessing* (Pocket Books, New York, 1989)

CHESTER MITCHELL holds a Bachelor of Arts Degree in Communications from Queens College of the City University of New York (1980). He also holds a Bachelor of Arts Degree in Theology from Christian Life College in Stockton, California (1984). Prior to his ministry in Virginia, he served from 1984-1996 as the Executive Pastor of Christian Life Center in Stockton under his mentor Bishop Kenneth F. Haney.

Pastor Mitchell's ministry has taken him across the United States, Canada, Australia, Great Britain, El Salvador, Haiti, and Jamaica, where he was born and raised before moving to the United States. He is the Lead Pastor of Capital Community Church in Ashburn, Virginia, which he and his wife, Marion, founded in 1996.

CONTACT CHESTER MITCHELL:

Capital Community Church
20430 Ashburn, Village Blvd.
Ashburn, VA 20147
(703) 858-3864

admin@chestermitchell.org
http://www.capitalcommunity.org

Twitter: @clloydmitchell
Facebook: Chester Mitchell Ministries

CHESTER MITCHELL MINISTRY RESOURCES:

http://www.chestermitchell.org/

Made in the USA
Charleston, SC
10 July 2013